Consumerism, Sustainability, and Happiness

What would it take to have a world where everyone had enough? How can we eliminate poverty, leave enough for nonhuman nature, and increase well-being? This book explores ways the reader can live their life, engage with cultural change, and engage with policy making, to build that world.

We are presently on a path to environmental destruction, as our societies are driven by forces which leave many people without what they need to meet their basic needs, while also wasting vast resources on an unsatisfying consumer economy. The current system does not lead to a sense of well-being, even among those who are relatively materially comfortable. This book focuses on solutions for building a world of enough. It explains how we can reorient our thinking and take the steps necessary to transform our social systems. It looks at ways to reduce the insatiable desire for status and consumption that drive our economies. It focuses on emerging approaches to economics that take well-being as their goal and explores the policies that are crucial for getting there, such as reducing inequality, investing in public goods, and reducing work time. The book arms the reader with a variety of tools for building a world where everyone has enough for a good life.

Cynthia Kaufman is the Director of the Vasconcellos Institute for Democracy in Action De Anza College and is the author of *Challenging Power, The Sea Is Rising and So Are We, Getting Past Capitalism,* and *Ideas for Action.*

"Cynthia Kaufman captures the essence of the intertwining crises that embroil our world: excessive and wasteful consumption patterns that fuel growing inequalities, political conflict, subjective feelings of emptiness, and the climate catastrophe that threatens life itself. She maps out a range of viable and achievable solutions capable of challenging structures of domination and ameliorating our plight. This book is a must read for those seeking answers to a range of pressing contemporary conundrums, one that will have relevance for years to come."

Ron Hayduk, *Professor of Political Science, San Francisco State University*

"In these dark times, Cynthia Kaufman's book, *Consumerism, Sustainability, and Happiness*, brilliantly illuminates a pathway to a better world. It is not an easy path; it goes through rough terrain and requires overcoming obstacles created by vested interests. But with her careful, calm, and hopeful arguments, Kaufman persuades us that it is a path that we must follow."

Fred Block, *Research Professor of Sociology, University of California, Davis*

"Philosopher Cynthia Kaufman helps us understand how our lives can be more complete with less. In another compelling book that combines ideas and practice, she makes changes in our living "standards" look as easy as they are essential. A must read for the perplexed as well as the committed."

Kathryn Sklar, *Author of Florence Kelley and the Nation's Work*

"Cynthia Kaufman's new book *Consumerism, Sustainability and Happiness: How to Build a World Where Everyone Has Enough* is exactly what we need in today's fight for climate and environmental justice. Kaufman's tactical approach is a breath of fresh air, providing practical solutions to not only help us live more sustainably as individuals, but also to push for the needed systemic change that will help us achieve a more just and livable future for all. Centering the topics of happiness, poverty, and environmental sustainability for what it would mean to have "enough" and feel satisfied in our lives, Kaufman emphasizes discourses that we need to see more popularized in mainstream and environmentalist circles: the centering of wellbeing, valuing people over profits, reducing work time, the causes and historical legacies of poverty, capitalist logics that keep us from achieving our best potential as a human species, and the fallacies of the overpopulation issue, to name a few. Importantly, Kaufman also stresses the significance of individual action as a way to create cultural change, while also eschewing narratives of individual consumer responsibility as the sole way to make systemic change. Indeed, this book makes transparent how powerful structural forces upheld by many institutions today can be challenged and held accountable. Kaufman's writing is clear, approachable, and boils down difficult concepts so that anyone can immediately start acting in more sustainable ways and challenge existing power structures so as to help bring about a just transition."

Belinda Ramírez, PhD, *Stanford University Civic, Liberal, and Global Education (COLLEGE) Fellow*

Consumerism, Sustainability, and Happiness

How to Build a World Where Everyone Has Enough

Cynthia Kaufman

NEW YORK AND LONDON

Designed cover image: Nicola Wheston

First published 2023
by Routledge
605 Third Avenue, New York, NY 10158

and by Routledge
4 Park Square, Milton Park, Abingdon, Oxon, OX14 4RN

Routledge is an imprint of the Taylor & Francis Group, an informa business

© 2023 Cynthia Kaufman

The right of Cynthia Kaufman to be identified as author of this work
has been asserted in accordance with sections 77 and 78 of the
Copyright, Designs and Patents Act 1988.

All rights reserved. No part of this book may be reprinted or
reproduced or utilised in any form or by any electronic, mechanical,
or other means, now known or hereafter invented, including
photocopying and recording, or in any information storage or retrieval
system, without permission in writing from the publishers.

Trademark notice: Product or corporate names may be trademarks
or registered trademarks, and are used only for identification and
explanation without intent to infringe.

Library of Congress Cataloging-in-Publication Data
Names: Kaufman, Cynthia C., 1960- author.
Title: Consumerism, sustainability, and happiness: how to build a world
where everyone has enough/Cynthia Kaufman.
Description: New York, NY: Routledge, 2023. | Includes bibliographical
references and index. |
Identifiers: LCCN 2022054641 (print) | LCCN 2022054642 (ebook) | ISBN
9781032408231 (hardback) | ISBN 9781032408224 (paperback) | ISBN
9781003354871 (ebook)
Subjects: LCSH: Social change. | Consumption (Economics) | Sustainability.
| Happiness. | Human ecology.
Classification: LCC HM831 .K38 2023 (print) | LCC HM831 (ebook) | DDC
303.4–dc23/eng/20221115
LC record available at https://lccn.loc.gov/2022054641
LC ebook record available at https://lccn.loc.gov/2022054642

ISBN: 978-1-032-40823-1 (hbk)
ISBN: 978-1-032-40822-4 (pbk)
ISBN: 978-1-003-35487-1 (ebk)

DOI: 10.4324/9781003354871

Typeset in Bembo
by KnowledgeWorks Global Ltd.

Thanks

Vanessa Whang, Carlos Davidson, Ron Hayduk,
Dan Fuchs, Delia McGrath, Michael Gibson,
Kitty Sklar, Fred Block, and Peter Loeb

Contents

	Introduction	1
1	Happiness, Poverty, Sustainability	3
2	The Psychology of Enough	24
3	Building a Life with Enough	36
4	Economics Based on Scarcity and Infinite Growth	54
5	Capitalism, Socialism, and Solidarity Economics	71
6	Eliminating Extreme Poverty and Developing an Economics for Enough	89
7	Policies and Politics to Get to a World of Enough	101
	Conclusion	125
	Works Cited	130
	Index	137

Introduction

This book started with me wondering if it was possible to live in a world that was sustainable, given how driven people seem to be toward consumerism. With the urgency of the climate crisis, the dire levels of poverty in the world, and the fact that so many people who consume quite a bit more than they need seem to always want more, I wondered what it would take to end up with a world of enough: enough for everyone to live well, enough to leave for the environment, and enough for people to ever feel that they had enough.

Is it possible to shift our priorities to ensuring that all people actually have enough, and foster the sense that enough is, in fact, enough? This book argues that the answer is yes. There are plenty of the things that meet our needs and promote happiness to go around for everyone. But there are serious structural barriers to getting to a world of enough. The forces that give resources to those who don't need them, and which feed our insatiable hunger for more, are deeply entrenched in human society. Transforming those deeply entrenched systems is not easy, and it requires a tremendous amount of organizing. We will be better positioned to do that organizing if we understand the forces we are up against, how they work on people's psyches, what keeps us from seeing them, and what structural social changes we need to fight for, in order to build a society where everyone has enough and also *feels* that they have enough.

We need to transform much in our social systems to get to the point where we can allocate resources such that everyone can have their needs met, and to increase well-being, while also staying within the ecological limits of the planet. Human society is doing an unbelievably bad job of that at present. Tremendous social energy and natural resources are dedicated to the treadmill of conspicuous consumption, which decades of research have shown has no positive impact on how well people are doing. At the same time, billions of people live in extreme poverty or live precariously on the edge of it. The climate crisis, the biodiversity crisis, and other ecological crises all require urgent action.

DOI: 10.4324/9781003354871-1

This book is dedicated to helping us find a way to a world of enough. Chapter 1 lays a general sketch of the problem. It investigates the causes of poverty, the impact of our acquisitive society on the natural environment, and the ways that acquisitiveness leads to unhappiness. Chapter 2 focuses on what we need to do to build a psychology of enough. It looks at research on what leads people who have comfortable lives to feel that they don't have enough, and what leads people to feeling satisfied. Chapter 3 explores the things people can do in how they live their lives that will help build support for a world of enough. Chapter 4 is a critique of mainstream economic thinking. Chapter 5 looks at alternative economic models of capitalism, socialism, and solidarity economics. Chapter 6 looks at ways to eliminate poverty and explores the ways to think about care for our home, *oikos*—the root of the word *economics*—to develop an approach to economics that supports a world of enough. Chapter 7 explores the policy initiatives we need to be working on to get to a world of enough. Finally, the conclusion pulls together the lessons and steps for action that follow from the rest of the book.

There are many people who don't have enough—that is, enough to survive. They need more to eat, better places to live, more medical care, a more secure future for themselves and their loved ones. And yet *their* need for enough is not what is driving our political and economic systems. Rather, those systems are largely being driven by a society based on the pursuit of profit. This profit-based system is wrapped up, in a variety of complex ways that we will explore, with responding to the insatiable hunger to consume of those living above the level of poverty. Our present social order is counterproductive to happiness, counterproductive to providing enough for the poor, and counterproductive for environmental sustainability.

Many people doing work on these issues already know what needs to be done to have sustainable economies. What is keeping us from getting to a world of enough are two things. One is the fact that our political systems have to a large extent been captured by elite interests which are running them for profit, rather than for meeting human and ecological needs. The other is, those systems are buttressed by ideas which make a society controlled by those interests seem normal and natural. This book is about how to reorient our thinking to help clarify the steps we need to take to take power back and get to a world of enough.

Chapter 1

Happiness, Poverty, Sustainability

I try to be happy, and I know that people like happy people, but so often I feel bored. Sometimes I indulge a little bit. A good glass of wine can give me that content, mellow, relaxed feeling. But that doesn't last very long. I go to parties. I do like to have fun. But I sometimes stop and wonder, what's the point?[1]

When I am with my family, and there is enough to eat, and we are telling stories and laughing, I feel that life is good. But how often are we not worried about having the basics? Why is it so hard to just have those simple things?

You people who are talking about human beings living well are dreaming. Human beings are the scourge of the earth. Wherever we go we destroy everything in our path. We have found the enemy and he is us. Human beings and a healthy planet are simply incompatible. Human beings are too greedy to ever feel like they have enough. That's why the only way for the biosphere to survive is for there to be a lot less of our miserable species.

We live in a world where tremendous resources are used to feed, create, and temporarily satisfy seemingly insatiable consumer desires. All around the world, much political and economic decision-making is driven by the imperatives unleashed by those desires. This situation is leading to three interrelated crises: a crisis of unhappiness, a crisis of poverty, and a crisis of environmental sustainability. This chapter explores the nature of these crises in order to lay the foundation for pathways to a world where there is enough: where people are not driven to insatiability, where no one is left in poverty, and where our environmental systems have enough capacity to provide a healthy matrix in which our species, and others, can thrive. It also explores some of the issues in each of these three areas to show that it is possible to have enough. The rest of the book maps out the forces getting in the way of a world of enough and pathways to overcoming those forces.

DOI: 10.4324/9781003354871-2

4 Happiness, Poverty, Sustainability

At the core of each of these axes of enough there are deeply entrenched forces driving us away from what, on the surface, seem like obvious solutions. Why can't we set economic policies such that human and ecological needs are prioritized over more frivolous things, like some people having fancy yachts? Why don't more people who have materially comfortable lives feel happy? Why do we keep running society in ways that destroy the atmosphere and drive other species to extinction? In each of these three axes of enough, the problem is driven, at least in part, by capitalism. At its core, capitalism is a process that puts profits over people and which dehumanizes whole sectors of our population and makes it seem that their suffering doesn't matter.[2] Capitalism from its beginning has always been racial capitalism. Colonialism and slavery were there at its founding. A core principle of capitalism is that we are each responsible for our own fate. Someone else's suffering and lack of access to the basic resources needed to live is not anyone's responsibility to deal with. As South African Archbishop, and anti-apartheid activist, Desmond Tutu argued, "We have allowed the interests of capital to outweigh the interests of human beings and our Earth."[3]

Beginning with the idea that capitalism, and the forms of dehumanization and exploitation that go along with it, is at the root of the problems we are looking at and could lead the reader to believe that the goal of this book to get to a world of enough may not be possible. According to a popular saying attributed to Frederic Jameson, "It is easier to imagine the end of the world than the end of capitalism." In my book *Getting Past Capitalism: History, Vision, Hope*, I argue that it is possible to build a world beyond capitalism and that we do so by engaging in much of the social change work many of us are already doing. Getting past capitalism does not require a great leap into a completely different social world than the one we actually inhabit. Some of the ways that people who are anti-capitalist think about what capitalism is, and how it works, have made it hard to think clearly about the work that needs to be done to build that other world. Some of the ways they think about the problem make the already hard task of getting past capitalism seem harder than it actually is.[4]

Many of those who are critical of capitalism see it as a highly integrated system that must be overthrown. The idea of "a system" encourages us to think of society as something like a machine where all the parts rely on each other. That gives rise to the idea that it might be able to be broken or "smashed" and that it must be replaced with a whole new social system. More helpful for thinking about social change is the metaphor of society as a fabric that must be rewoven. The different parts are all connected, but there is no core part that must be transformed to have a different society. We build the new society, piece by piece. We get rid of the old, piece by piece. If we think of a society dominated by capitalism this way, we can see it as a variety of things that need to be challenged.

Capitalism is an underlying and widespread set of ideas, as well as a variety of practices, that support and are supported by those ideas. Just as those of us who challenge racism or gender-based oppression know that we need to fight on many fronts to make progress on challenging the social ills we are looking at, similarly with capitalism, we are better able to see clear pathways to action for liberation when we understand our opponent to be made up of a variety of things to be challenged in a variety of ways, rather than as a unified system to be overthrown.[5]

While discussions of capitalism inevitably lead to the questions of what can replace it, my main argument in this book is that we can push back in a variety of ways on the dominance of capitalist ideas and institutions and that we make the world better at every step as we do. How far toward an anti-capitalist world we need to go, and at what point do other problems arise and need to be dealt with, are issues I address in depth in *Getting Past Capitalism*. For the argument here, it is enough to look at the specific ideas and social practices that are leading us away from a world of enough and to argue for the specific things that get us to a world of enough. None of this is to say that getting past capitalism, and to a world of enough, is easy. The point, rather, is to understand what we are up against with more clarity and specificity, so that we can at least see the pathways to a better world.

Getting to a world of enough will require that we expose the ways that pro-capitalist thinking is woven deeply into much of how most of us understand our world, from how we think about markets, to how we think about freedom, to the ways we measure the success of our economies. Getting to a world of enough requires that we expose, and escape from, those ways of thinking. It requires that we take away power from those who are profiting from social processes bent on destruction. And it requires that we challenge and shift the social policies that hold up the practices that are supported by those ideas and those power structures. We need to rapidly shift to organizing society in ways that put meeting ecological and human needs above all else.

When addressing the issues of housing, for example, we need to ask what can lead to a world where everyone has a decent place to live, and we need to pursue the policies that lead to that result. When looking at why people are so driven to wasteful consumerism, we need to look at the social forces that drive people toward insatiability, and we need to work to shift those forces. When looking at what is keeping us from ending reliance of fossil fuels, we need to look at the forces that are slowing progress to a stable climate. Each social problem we face has a set of solutions that need to be pursued. Even though capitalism can be understood as a driving force underneath all of those problems, we can address the problems individually, even as we understand how they are interrelated. To the extent that we can shift our political systems to meet human needs and ecological needs, we have a world less dominated by capitalism.

6 Happiness, Poverty, Sustainability

A large part of the current dominant way of understanding the world indicates that people are basically greedy and always want more and that the best society is one that feeds that desire. It argues that allowing people to pursue profit above all else will lead to more being produced and so it will give people what they want. And it argues that because more stuff is produced more "efficiently," fewer people will live in poverty. It argues that "economic growth" is good for everyone, that a rising tide lifts all boats. It argues that if people try, they can get what they need.

Dominant pro-capitalist narratives tend to be silent on the environmental crises we face. When they speak about them at all, they ask consumers to vote with their dollars by buying greener products if they want a greener world. Getting to a world of enough will require that we get outside of that way of thinking. When we see the weaknesses in that framework and have other ways of understanding how human beings and human society work, we are in a better position to advocate for different social, political, and economic practices.

This chapter looks at three axes of enough: happiness, poverty, and environmental sustainability, to show what in our current world is keeping us from getting to a place where everyone has enough. The section on happiness argues against the dominant view that consumerism and increased Gross Domestic Product (GDP) in a given country lead to happiness. The section on poverty argues that there is plenty of material wealth in the world for everyone to have enough and that something as simple as a better distribution of resources, even within the current economic structure, can solve the problem of poverty. The section on the environment argues that we can live sustainably and well, with current technologies, and that we can get there in the time needed to avert the worst of the climate and biodiversity crises. Later chapters look at practical ways to realize those goals.

Happiness

In *Happiness in World History*, Peter Stearns tracks the increase in uses of the term *happiness* in print in the English and shows an accelerating interest in the idea starting in the 18th century.[6] The idea that a goal of human life was to be happy is very much associated with the current period. It is in many ways related to capitalism and consumer culture. The form of happiness most associated with the pleasures promoted by consumer culture is captured in the Greek term *hedonism*, which refers to the pleasures of the body.

When that sort of happiness is pursued as the goal of life, it is easy for that pursuit to backfire. A person who lives with pleasure as their main goal often doesn't pay enough attention to relationships and the practical matters of life. And so, the pleasure often doesn't last very long. We all know stories of people who pursue lives of pleasure, who eat too much, become addicted to drugs, or act selfishly in their relationships with others and end up very unhappy or dying early. And, as many people in contemporary consumerist societies find, a life led primarily for the purpose of consumer pleasure can end up feeling empty and meaningless.

This approach to happiness is often contrasted with an approach that focuses instead on the Greek concept of *eudaimonia*, which refers to a life well lived. It literally means "good spirit" and it encompasses well-being, flourishing, and happiness. The concept was central to Aristotle's ethics. For him a virtuous person was a person who lived well in their relations with others, and was therefore happy in a broad sense. A person with *eudaimonia* is a person who is well regarded by others, holding up their part of social relationships, and is content with the way they are living their life.

This view is in accord with the ideas of the good life in many different cultural traditions. The Chinese systems of Daoism and Confucianism focus on a life lived in balance and harmony with others, with the whole of the universe, and with society as a whole. Buddhism teaches the eightfold path to a good life, which involves self-restraint and kindness to others. A core underlying philosophical premise of many traditional African societies is the concept of *ubuntu*, "I am because we are," which expresses the importance of living well with others to the well-being of a person.[7] One expression of this widespread idea is in the Sotho saying, "a person is a person through persons."[8] *Buen vivir*, or living well, came to international attention as an ideal when it was embedded in the Ecuadorian constitution in 2008, which also gave rights to nature. *Buen vivir* is a Spanish translation of a Quecha term *sumak kawsay*, and it stresses living in harmony with all living beings, and with a balance of the material and spiritual aspects of life.[9] Many societies in the world, going back a long way in human history, have concepts of the good life that encourage us to see well-being and a life well lived, as something that matters, and as something more than a life of pleasure.

In their book *How Much is Enough: Money and the Good Life*, Robert and Edward Skidelsky argue that in the modern world we are "heirs to a conceptual revolution" that has shrunk the meaning of happiness to nothing but private pleasure. They argue that "eudaimonia, the Greek work conventionally translated as 'happiness' does not refer to a state of *mind* at all, but to an admirable and desirable state of *being*. It is a matter of public appraisal, not private awareness." The Skidelsky's worry is that current conversations about what makes people happy have fallen prey to the shallow hedonistic approach.[10] There are good philosophical reasons to question shallow forms of happiness as the goal of life.

Asking what makes people happy is also complicated by the fact that in some countries, such as the US, being happy is an important sign of success. And so, people will overreport their level of happiness and feel pressurized to be cheerful.[11] In many Asian countries, a life well lived is associated with fulfilling one's obligations to others and with self-restraint. Focusing on one's

8 Happiness, Poverty, Sustainability

own happiness can be seen as anti–social and shallow. Stearns reports on a Russian adage that says, "a person who smiles too much is either a fool or an American."[12] And so, by focusing on happiness, are we falling prey to the cultural dynamics that drive consumer capitalism? To ask what people need to live well, should we even be asking about what makes them happy?

There is an emerging social scientific literature on happiness, which tries to navigate these problems by starting with a very thin definition of happiness. Researchers have asked people from a wide variety of countries, and across social classes, questions such as "overall, how is your life?" And "are you satisfied with your life?" Without digging too deeply into the question of what makes a live well lived, the happiness literature has given powerful resources for helping us get to a world of enough. These studies of happiness are important, not because they take happiness to be the goal of human existence, but because they go to the bottom of dominant ways of thinking and turn that thinking on its head. They challenge dominant beliefs about the relationships among consumption, economic growth, and happiness. If we want to get to a world of enough, it is important to attend to what makes people feel that their lives are good. There are many powerful insights emerging from the research into happiness that are helpful for understanding what it will take to get to a world of enough.

A huge part of an individual's happiness is personal and is not related to social forces at all, but rather may be an inborn temperament. Stearns quotes psychologists who claim that this inborn aspect of happiness may account for around 50% of an individual's happiness.[13] But when looked at as a social average, the results on what kinds of social order lead to a higher general level of happiness are remarkably consistent.

The social scientific literature on happiness is practically unanimous in finding that total levels of happiness in a given society are higher when that society offers conditions that allow high levels of trust, a sense of security for one's future and the future of one's family, and a sense of belonging. There is more happiness in societies with lower levels of inequality and higher levels of social cohesion. And while inequality undermines social cohesion, there are subcultures within any society that can have stronger than average levels of cohesion and therefore of happiness.

Social scientific research on happiness has shed a lot of light on the complex relationships among wealth, inequality, GDP, and happiness. In his book *Happiness: Lessons from a New Science*, Richard Layard argued that beyond a very low level of having one's basic needs met, which globally is $10,000 per year, a society with more wealth has no more happiness than a society with less. A more unequal society has lower levels of happiness than one with more equality. The US, a society that is very wealthy and very stratified by race and class, has the same average level of happiness as Costa Rica, a country with low levels of inequality, much less per capita wealth, and a much lower level of per capita greenhouse gas emissions. In a society with high levels of inequality, those at the top are generally, on average, happier than those lower down.[14] But research has shown that status anxiety is higher, even for those at the top, in highly unequal societies, than it is for people lower down in relatively egalitarian societies.[15]

But, in a society with a high level of inequality, having more does, on average, make a person happier than a person who has less. It isn't the stuff that makes you happier. Rather, in a stratified society, having more stuff than other people makes you happier than them. In other words, happiness is related to status, and in an unequal modern materialist society, status is related to having more and better things than others.[16]

On some level many of us intuitively know that money doesn't make one happy and that it is better to pursue other things in life. And yet the economies of most countries take as their main measure of success increases in GDP. GDP measures the level of economic activity, defined as goods and services being bought and sold. Taking GDP as the most important measure of an economy implies that the most important goal of a nation's economy is to produce more economic throughput.

Layard argues that GDP was not intended by its creators to measure the overall health of an economy. It was originally created to help predict and manage boom and bust cycles within an economy.[17] Over time it has come to be used as a general measure of economic health. That is partly because it measures what is of interest to the wealthy and powerful. An economy that generates more buying and selling *is* a better economy for them.

But as generations of feminist economists have pointed out, GDP measures "bads" as much as it measures goods. A hurricane that destroys a city, and so that city needs to spend a tremendous of money cleaning up, will have its GDP boosted by the hurricane. GDP completely ignores all of the important things we do to take care of our needs outside the realm of buying and selling. A society where people worked 20 hours a week, cooked for each other, shared child care and elder care, and made things for the fun of it would have much higher levels of happiness and health than one in which people worked 80-hour weeks and paid for all of those things. The later society would have a much higher carbon footprint and higher levels of stress. And it would have a much higher GDP.[18]

In the US, the size of houses doubled between the years 1970 and 2010, but the level of happiness has stayed the same.[19] There is a dramatic and devastating shortage of housing available for people with low and moderate incomes. There was a time when the US government and private business invested in building housing for people who did not have a lot of wealth or income. There were single room occupancy hotels, government-subsidized apartment complexes, and many developers building small homes. But none of those things led to high levels of profits for anyone. And so, as the government has stopped supporting the building those sorts of homes, not enough of them are being built. Many people say that there is not enough money to pay school teachers well, to invest in public transportation, or in green technology. And yet as a society, the US spends tremendous social resources building mansions. Social resources are going to feed the insatiable engine of profit.

There are two important factors that impact happiness which matter for social policy: one is socioeconomic inequality and the other is social cohesion, or a sense of belonging. Inequality reduces social solidarity and makes it harder for people to advocate in a political system for the material things that lead to happiness, such as secure access to income, education, and stable housing, and financial stability in old age. In many societies, being a part of a racial minority means that one is likely subjected to higher levels of socioeconomic insecurity, and these decrease levels of happiness.

And yet, these class impacts of race do not tell the whole story. It turns out that belonging is an important part of happiness, and racial minorities are likely to not experience a sense of belonging in the dominant culture. But paradoxically, they may inhabit subcultures that are less destroyed by the dominant culture of competitive individualism. In some cases, there are higher levels of happiness in some communities of color in the US, than among members of the dominant white group. In the US, generally white people are happier than Black people. But an interesting finding is that among the very old, Black people are happier than white people. This paradoxical finding has been explained as resulting from stronger social bonds among elderly Black people in the US than among elderly white people in the US.[20]

According to a study by Fengyan Tang et al., "Black older Americans are at least as satisfied as, and even happier than White peers, indicating the absence of disparities in emotional wellbeing."[21]

Studies have shown similar results within Latinx cultures in the US. Research on health outcomes shows a

> "Hispanic health paradox" which finds higher than expected levels of a variety of health and well-being indicators among Latinx groups, given their otherwise lower rankings on socio-economic indicators typically associated with positive outcomes. This literature has often pointed to a stronger sense of family, community, religion, and group identity as the cultural factors driving the paradox in health and well-being outcomes.[22]

This data on Black and Latinx cultures in the US points to cultural assets that exist on these communities that should be taken into account when thinking about ways to increase happiness in a society. Increasing happiness in society involves increasing those aspects of our social world that lead to higher senses of belonging and security. And it involves fighting against inequality. In highly unequal societies, people are unhappy for a number of reasons. They worry about their ability to meet their basic needs. They worry about their futures and the future for their loved ones. And in unequal societies, political inequality leads to policies that favor the already well off and encourage politicians to feed off of social division to win elections.

In *How Much is Enough: Money and the Good Life*, Robert and Edward Skidelsky criticize the social scientific literature on happiness for focusing on happiness as the goal of life. They worry that a society could increase its overall level of happiness by doing things like putting everyone on the drug soma, which, in the dystopian novel *Brave New World*, made everyone happy while leaving them with no higher passions, consciousness, or purpose in life.[23] For the Skidelskys, the good life, rather than happiness, is what we should all be aiming at.

And yet the social science of happiness really does not make that mistake, and does not reduce happiness to hedonism. The researchers don't ask people if they feel joy and euphoria. Rather, they ask more open questions, such as if they are satisfied with their lives. The approach in this research does not require an investigation of whether or not people are thinking of hedonism, eudaimonia, the eightfold path, *ubuntu*, or *buen vivir*, when asked about their well-being. The skeletal concept of happiness in the happiness literature is good enough to make the points that this literature has successfully achieved. Without making too many normative claims about how people should live, it helps us challenge the notion that more spending is what should be driving our economic decisions.

The happiness literature has laid a powerful foundation for the claim that our societies should be aiming to provide enough for everyone to live well. It helps us reject the idea that we need to have our economies oriented to the goal of economic growth and increased production, if those things don't lead to satisfying the basic needs of the poor, or the psychological needs of almost anyone. The happiness literature helps us to see that there is something radically wrong in a society that devotes tremendous resources to producing ever more wasteful goods that destroy the environment, while leaving people, in both wealthy and poor countries, in poverty, and which don't lead to happiness.

Poverty

In a world where every year enough food is produced to feed everyone well, millions of people are chronically malnourished. In the US, where houses are doubling in size, more than half a million people don't have homes on any given night. We don't have poverty because there isn't enough. We have poverty because of the ways our resources are distributed.

According to John Iceland, there are two general ways of looking at poverty: absolute and relative. Absolute poverty is typically defined as being "without adequate shelter, clothes, or food." Relative measures of poverty, however, "define poverty as a condition of comparative disadvantage, to be accessed against some relative, shifting, or evolving standard of living."[24] Absolute poverty is a situation where someone does not have their basic physical needs met. Relative poverty is where they don't have what is necessary to live as a full member of the society in which they live. A cell phone is needed to not be poor in the US. In many places, so is a car. But cars and cell phones are not basic necessities. Poverty is produced by a society generating ways of living that are crucial for feeling oneself to be a full member of society, while not having mechanisms for providing those things for all people.

In the *Affluent Society*, John Kenneth Galbraith argued that

> people are poverty-stricken whenever their income, even if adequate for survival, falls markedly behind that of the community. Then they cannot have what the larger community regards as the minimum necessary for decency; and they cannot wholly escape, therefore, the judgement of the larger community that they are indecent.[25]

People in the low-wealth, high happiness, country of Bhutan don't need cars to live like their neighbors. People in suburban California do. People have gone for millennia without the internet. But once using it becomes the way to get by, and do all of the things that we are expected to do, access becomes a necessity. During the COVID-19 pandemic, in San José California, volunteers were giving homeless people small solar panels for their cell phones, because the usual places where they charged their phones were closed. In the Silicon Valley having a cell phone is necessary for being connected to others in ways that make life work. Eliminating poverty requires that we address both absolute and relative poverty. We need to ensure that people have access to what they need to meet their basic physical needs, and what they need to meet their social needs.

When we look at the question of poverty globally, there are millions of people, in both rich and poor countries, who don't just not have what their society requires for them to be full participants; they don't even have what is required for basic human health. All around the world, people are suffering from high rates of absolute poverty. Finding ways to eliminate absolute poverty should be one of the most urgent goals of social policy. This is especially true as the climate crisis undermines the access to livelihood for millions of people, especially in the impoverished countries in the global south. People in the poorer countries in Latin America, Asia, Africa, and small island nations have done the least to cause the climate crisis, yet they are locked out of the possibility of moving to places in the world that are livable, as the global north uses immigration policies to create fortresses to keep them out.

The mainstream view, dominant in institutions such as the World Bank and International Monetary Fund, is that the way to eliminate poverty is to stimulate more economic growth. As the metaphor goes: growth is the rising tide that can lift all boats. And yet much research has shown that increases in GDP do little to eliminate poverty. Economic growth means that more things are bought and sold in a country, but it says nothing about how the money generated by that buying and selling is distributed or spent. To eliminate poverty, poor people need access to money, or to other means of satisfying their needs. The total level of buying and selling going on around them doesn't give that to them. And sometimes as more money comes into an area, poverty rates go up, as there is more competition for necessities such as housing.

Christopher Lakner and his co-authors did an analysis that compared the impact of growth on poverty with the impact of inequality reduction. They found that reducing inequality has a much bigger impact on poverty reduction than does economic growth.[26] A recent Oxfam report argues that global inequality has reached the point where the "world's billionaires have more wealth than 4.6 billion people."[27] The focus on growth as a way to eliminate poverty feeds the very machine of profit-driven production and consumption which is destroying environment, and leading to lives of insatiability. And there is no evidence that it helps reduce poverty.

In his final report after finishing his work as the United Nations (UN) official in charge of leading the Sustainable Development Goals process with respect to poverty reduction, Philip Alston argues that poverty is a political choice. There is plenty in the world to meet the needs of everyone. There can be debates about the right level of inequality needed to keep a society producing enough for everyone to live well. Socialists argue that we can have well-functioning societies with virtually no inequality. Pro-capitalist thinkers argue that inequality helps spur economic ingenuity. We will dig more deeply into those questions in later chapters. For now, we don't need to enter into those debates to see a simple solution to the problem of absolute poverty, what the UN refers to as extreme poverty.

It would take a very small level of redistribution to completely eliminate extreme poverty. This can easily be done, Alston argues, with small increases in taxation:

> Extreme poverty is and must be understood as a violation of human rights. Protestations of inadequate resources are entirely unconvincing given the determined refusal of many governments to adopt just fiscal policies, end tax evasion, and stop corruption. Poverty is a political choice and will be with us until its elimination is reconceived as a matter of social justice.[28]

In most countries in the world, living below that basic level of $10,000 per year means that one is not meeting one's basic needs. Finding ways to ensure that everyone in the world has that floor below them should be the highest priority of economic policy. Beyond that floor of extreme poverty, the story becomes more complicated. In countries with rising inequality, people's well-being can go down even as their material living standard goes up, because their decrease in absolute poverty can be paired with a rise in relative poverty. We eliminate poverty by orienting social systems to ensure that everyone has access to what they need to be considered full members of their society. Strategies for eliminating absolute poverty are explored in Chapter 6. Taxing the wealthy and eliminating tax avoidance are important for generating the revenue to provide for the basic needs everyone needs to avoid extreme poverty. Chapter 2 explores the ways that inequality leads to increases in relative poverty. Chapter 7 explores ways to use taxation to minimize inequality and reduce both forms of poverty.

The Environmental Crisis

In addition to undermining the roots of happiness and leading to poverty, the current system that dominates the world is also devastating to the matrix of natural systems on which our lives depend. We are facing looming crises of biodiversity loss, ocean acidification, fresh water scarcity, pollution, and climate change. All of these crises need to be addressed, urgently. Many of the things done to solve one will generally be helpful for addressing the others. Preserving forests because they sequester carbon, also preserves bio-diversity. Limiting the sale of throwaway plastics addresses a few problems: it lessens water and land pollution, and because plastics are made with fossil fuels, reducing their use also lowers emissions.

The scientists have been very clear that we need to reduce our greenhouse gas emissions to 50% below 2020 levels by 2030 and to zero by 2050.[29] We also need to preserve approximately 30% of the world's land mass by 2030 and 50% by 2050 to leave enough for other species to thrive, and to prevent the spread of zoonotic diseases.[30] To achieve those goals, we need to completely remove fossil fuels from our economies, we need to stop destroying forests and allow them to regenerate, and we need to reorient our societies to being more resilient to the disasters that are inevitable, given the level of damage that has already been done.[31]

At present there are three major approaches to making those things happen: techno-optimism, neo-Malthusianism, and environmental justice. The techno-optimists believe that with currently developing technologies, all of our environmental problems can be addressed, without requiring much deep social change or painful struggle. Governments need to add a few more regulations to make clean technologies economically more competitive in the market with dirty technologies. Governments need to subsidize those technologies. Businesses and consumers need to support innovation. Bill Gates, Michael Bloomberg, and Carl Pope have written books that tout the ability of smart business practices, good technology, and consumer choice, to solve the climate crisis.[32] These thinkers believe that there is easily enough for all, if we just nudge society toward smarter choices.

On the opposite side of the spectrum are the neo-Malthusians who believe that no matter how much we embrace new technologies, there is not enough for the seven billion people who currently inhabit the planet to live sustainably, and there is certainly not enough for the ten-billion-person population we are likely to have as global populations level off later this century. They argue that we can only get to a world of enough with a drastic reduction in the size of the human population. Advocates of environmental justice argue that we can get to a sustainable world for ten-billion people, but that we will need to fight against entrenched powers to get there.

Neo-Malthusianism has fallen out of favor in recent years, but strains of it persist to this day. In the 1970s and 1980s, it was a dominant school of environmental thought. In his 1798 book, *An Essay on the Principle of Population*, Thomas Malthus argued that populations have a tendency to expand exponentially, while the food supply only increases in a linear fashion. His conclusion from that was that there was no point trying to solve the problem of poverty, because if you feed people, they will reproduce more, just creating more poor people. Of course, Malthus has been proven wrong by history: human society has always produced enough food to feed everyone. Hunger is caused by political systems that keep that food from getting to the people who need it. Poverty is not an inevitable aspect of human society.[33]

Since Malthus' time, many thinkers have taken up his banner and have argued for reduced population as a way to deal with the overuse of resources. They have focused on population reduction as a core part of environmentalism. And in almost every case, they have focused on the populations of the global south as the ones that need reducing. In a 1986 interview, Earth First! founder Dave Forman said, "The worst thing we can do in Ethiopia [during a famine] is to send aid—the best thing would be just to let nature seek its own balance and let people there just starve."[34]

In their 1968 book *The Population Bomb*, Paul and Ann Ehrlich set off alarm bells across the world that overpopulation was going to cause massive starvation and ecological crises. In that book, the authors approve of the strategy advocated by William and Paul Paddock whereby "Rich nations should send all their food aid to those poor countries that still had some hope of one day feeding themselves; hopeless countries like India and Egypt should be cut off immediately." The Ehrlichs wrote, "there is no rational choice except to adopt some form of the Paddocks' strategy as far as food distribution is concerned."[35] As recently as 2013, Anne and Paul Ehrlich wrote an article that claims that overpopulation has been a more significant contributor to the climate crisis than overconsumption.[36]

One of the more widely respected current neo-Malthusian thinkers is William Rees. Rees argues that most approaches to the climate and ecological crises are looking for solutions in the wrong places. He doesn't believe in

16 Happiness, Poverty, Sustainability

renewable energy (RE) as a solution because those technologies rely on fossil fuels, and an extractive economy, to be produced. And they can never get us to the point where human beings can live within the biophysical limits of the planet, because RE carriers, "are impossible to scale up in a climate-relevant time-frame.[37] Because those technological solutions will not work, he argues that we need, "a global population strategy to enable a smooth, socially just descent to the one to two billion people that could live comfortably indefinitely without destroying the ecosphere."[38]

Rees and his colleague Megan Seibert published a paper criticizing the scientific literature on the mainstream approaches to getting to a sustainable future. In it they argue that the only solution is drastic and rapid population reduction.[39] They write:

> We cannot stress enough that a non-fossil energy regime simply cannot support anywhere close to the present human population of nearly eight billion; this urgently necessitates reducing human numbers as rapidly as possible to avoid unprecedented levels of social unrest and human suffering in the coming decades.[40]

There are two parts to their argument that are worth addressing, in order to look at the question of whether or not we can get to a world of enough. One is whether or not we need to push for extreme population reduction as a solution to the environmental crises we face. The other is the question of the feasibility of technological solutions to support a large population. Can we get to a sustainable world where everyone has enough, without taking drastic measures on population, or giving up modern lifestyles?

On the question of population, Seibert and Rees take pains to argue for a "socially just and humane" approach to population reduction. And yet, in line with most neo-Malthusians' tendency to look at controlling the lives of far-away others when discussing population, Seibert and Rees argue that population reduction strategies should be focused on "high-fertility countries."[41] What is troubling about this is that "high-fertility countries" are also countries with very low per capita environmental impacts. Those are not the countries that are driving our environmental crises.

According to George Monbiot:

> Between 1980 and 2005, for instance, sub-Saharan Africa produced 18.5% of the world's population growth and just 2.4% of the growth in CO_2. North America turned out only 4% of the extra people, but 14% of the extra emissions. Sixty-three percent of the world's population growth happened in places with very low emissions.[42]

In making their case for a socially just approach to population reduction, Seibert and Rees rely on the work of Colin Hickey, Travis N. Rieder, and

Jake Earl. Those authors argue that reducing population should be a part of the wide variety of approaches taken to address the climate crisis. They advocate increased access to family planning services, education for women, advertising campaigns promote the value of fewer children, as well as economic incentives, such as paying for birth control, or removing tax incentives for having more children. They point out that many countries in the world have in place "pronatalist policies" that intentionally promote higher birth rates and that some of those policies are not helpful to low-income women and children. In most cases, they are in place to serve reactionary forms of ethno-nationalism. The authors point to the coercive policies promoted in the recent past by China, India, and Singapore as morally unacceptable.

In a widely cited paper in *Science*, on population reduction and the climate, Eileen Crist et al. argue, in alignment with Hickey et al., that a smaller population puts less stress on resources and that there are other social benefits that come from humane approaches to reducing the population.

> Wherever human rights–promoting policies to lower fertility rates have been implemented, birth rates have declined within a generation or two. Policies include prominent public discourse on the issue; prioritizing the education of girls and women; establishing accessible and affordable family planning services; provisioning modern contraceptive methods through diverse outlets; deploying health workers for grassroots education and support; making counseling for couples available; eliminating governmental incentives for large families; and making sexuality education mandatory in school curricula.[43]

While Seibert and Rees focus on "high fertility countries" as the places to do the work of population reduction, Hickey et al. very specifically do not. They acknowledge the higher impact of lower birth rates in high wealth countries, given the higher environmental impacts of individuals in those countries. And in a paper published after the one cited by Rees and Seibert, they argue for increased migration to solve the economic problems that might arise from the graying populations in the global north. "Supplementing fertility reduction with policies that facilitate the emigration of younger people from developing nations to developed nations could allow for both global reductions in GHG emissions and continued economic stability."[44]

There is nothing wrong with supporting the humane policies that also lead to lower birth rates. Taking a measured and humanitarian approach to the issue, the authors of *Drawdown* write, "when family planning focuses on healthcare provision and meeting women's expressed needs, empowerment, equality, and well-being are the goal; benefits to the planet are side effects."[45] Population goes down as women have more power and people's lives have some stability.

18 Happiness, Poverty, Sustainability

As of this writing, demographers believe that world population is likely to level of by 2050 at ten billion people. Crist et al. believe that the empowering policies mentioned above could get the world on target for a leveling off mid-century at 8.7 billion people.[46] None of these thinkers believes that humane policies can get you to the population of 1–2 billion that Seibert and Rees say is required for a healthy environment.

While many neo-Malthusians express deep frustration at the silence in the climate movement around population, they have themselves to blame for that silence. Population has become a taboo subject among people working for a sustainable world because those focusing on its importance have tended to favor racist and draconian approaches. Their proposals invariably target population reduction schemes toward the bodies of those least responsible for the ecological crises we face. The loudest voices for population reduction have in most cases taken an explicitly, or in the cases of Seibert and Rees, implicitly racist approach to the issue.

If those arguing for "drastic and rapid reduction in birth rates" focused on policies that encouraged migration from the global south to the global north to balance labor needs, or if they focused on abortion and contraception rights for people in the global north, their ideas might be met with less skepticism. And as the following section shows, Seibert and Rees produced a bad faith argument about the inability of technology to support a larger population in order to buttress their conclusion that we need to limit the fertility of people in the global south.

A group of scientists working on sustainable technology published a response to Seibert and Rees' paper. In it they go through each of Seibert and Rees' claims and show the paper to be based on "an unacceptable non-scientific approach that includes selective (and hence biased) screening of the literature focusing on the challenges related to technologically enabled renewable energy solutions, without discussing any of the proposed solutions." They go on to write that "Seibert and Rees adopt the fatalistic and unimaginative perspective" whereby "just 1 billion people would inhabit the Earth, due to a forced reduction of population."[47] The authors conclude that "It is unfortunate, counterproductive, and ethically deplorable that the authors turn a legitimate discussion of the challenges of defossilizing the global economy into a political diatribe."[48]

There is a near consensus among the scientists who study the subject that there are technical pathways to a world where ten billion people can live well and stay within the biophysical limits of the planet's environmental systems. Mark Jacobson has done some of the most important, empirically grounded, work gathering together existing literature on the subject, and doing his own studies, to show how quick adoption of existing technologies can get us to sustainability and high levels of human well-being at projected population levels.[49] Jacobson's work does not get into the question of the political barriers to adopting those sustainable practices. He is neither a techno-optimist nor an advocate of environmental justice. His work is focused only on the tough questions of which technologies should be adopted to get us to sustainability.

Arguing that a sustainable world at ten billion is still possible is not the same as saying that it will be easy to get there or that we actually *will* get there. In contrast to the techno-optimists, advocates of environmental justice argue that markets themselves will not lead to the adoption of sustainable ways of meeting society's needs in the incredibly short time frames needed. The 25 major fossil fuel companies responsible for 71% of global emission since 1988 are fighting to the death to be able to continue to profit from their deadly products.[50] They are also fighting for a continued use of throwaway plastics and agriculture based on nitrogen fertilizers, both of which are fossil fuel based. Agribusiness continues to destroy the Amazon basin. Fossil fuel companies are working to rip through one of the most biologically sensitive areas of the world, the Congo Basin, with the East Africa Crude Oil Pipeline.[51]

Only a political fight to take away the power from those profiting from the earth's destruction will get us to the sustainable society; scientists like Jacobson show us it is possible. If we have democratic societies that take environmental devastation seriously, we can find ways to make batteries with minimal damage to the environment and to the communities that live near where materials are mined. Mining can largely be replaced by mandated systems of recycling. Clean energy is already cheaper to build than fossil-fuel based energy. The world's food systems can be made sustainable by lowering meat and dairy consumption and growing food with more sustainable practices. As I argue in *The Sea is Rising and so are We*, almost all of the changes that need to be made will make the lives of most of us better rather than worse.[52]

What is slowing our progress toward the crucial goal of a sustainable society are political systems that are controlled by fossil fuel interests, banks that support those interests, and those wishing to profit from our consumer lifestyles. For decades, the fossil fuel industry has spent hundreds of millions of dollars sowing confusion and doubt about the climate crisis. They succeeded in slowing down action for 30 crucial years. And at this late date, when we need to reduce global emissions beginning immediately, and continuing at a sharp pace for the next 30 years, there are still many banks, pension systems, and investment funds which are pouring money into the development of fossil fuel infrastructure and funding deforestation. Governments all around the world are still subsidizing the fossil fuel industry at the rate of over $4 trillion dollars a year, $649 billion of that from the US.[53] Most countries are, to greater or lesser extents, still allowing the profit motive, and the interests of those with capital drive important social decisions.

A society driven by the profit motive will incentivize wasteful forms of consumerism. If it is cheap for a phone manufacturer to buy newly mined rare earth metals for phones and have us by a new phone every few years, they are going to make disposable phones that put those metals, which are mined

20 Happiness, Poverty, Sustainability

with so much human and ecological pain, into landfills. Only when there are rules in place that force companies to take responsibility for the disposal of their products, will their incentive to produce for the trash can be eliminated. And as long as it makes a person feel socially successful to have a new phone every year, people will keep buying and disposing of phones.

Most of the world is dominated by capitalist ways of understanding the world and is run by pro-capitalist politicians. Those politicians do the bidding of the companies that would like to have us keep on buying those things that add to their wealth. The logic of profit maximization drives our political systems. Politicians are elected on the basis of one dollar one vote, and the corporations that profit from our current wasteful lifestyles us are the ones with the most dollars to spend.

The dominant approach that is destroying the environment is also propped up by the discipline of economics, which teaches that more economic growth, and thus a higher GDP, means a better world for all of us and that we need to consume so that others can have jobs. Wasteful consumerism is propped up by the hedonic treadmill, which leads many people to choose politicians who promise them bigger homes, more stuff, and increased GDP. That problem is explored in Chapter 2 and solutions to it are explored in Chapter 3. Building a world where we can stay within the ecological limits of the planet requires that we stop putting social resources into the things that are destroying the planet without actually making people feel that they are living well.

Conclusion

Having important social decisions be driven by insatiability and profit is leading to environmental devastation, poverty, and low levels of happiness. Making a shift toward a sustainable society involves freeing people from the pulls that tie them to a need for more, and it involves advocating for policies that will invest in the things that meet human and ecological needs.

We need to figure out how to build popular support for a politics that strives to ensure that everyone has enough to live well, while staying with the ecological limits of the planet. We need to make the case that as we shift toward a world of enough, people will actually be happier. One of the hardest things we are up against in making that case is that our culture is saturated with ways of experiencing the world that tell us the opposite, that we need bigger homes, fancier cars, and the latest thing. Dealing with that problem is the subject of Chapter 2.

A few lessons from this:

1 Inequality leads to lower levels of happiness in a society.
2 The main things needed to increase happiness are security that one's needs, and the needs of loved ones are met, a sense of belonging, and a sense of security.

3 Economic growth does not reduce poverty. Poverty is reduced when poor people have access to the resources they need to live well. Small amounts of economic redistribution can eliminate absolute poverty.
4 The technologies already exist to address with the ecological crises we face. Getting widespread adoption of those technologies will require a political fight against the fossil fuel industry, which is dedicated to slowing that progress.
5 There is enough in the world for everyone to live well within the ecological limits required for healthy eco-systems. That is true, even if the world ends up with the 8.7 to 10-billion-person population we are likely to have as population levels off around 2050.

Notes

1 These statements, when they don't have a separate footnote, are made up and are intended to represent the kinds of things people say on the subject of the chapter.
2 On the origins of racism in capitalism see: Michael Omi and Howard Winant. 2014. *Racial Formation in the United States.* Routledge. On the concept of racial capitalism, see Cedric Robinson. 1983. *Black Marxism: The Making of the Black Radical Tradition.* Zed Press.
3 Desmond Tutu. "We Need an Apartheid Style Boycott to Save the Planet." April 10, 2014, *The Guardian.*
4 Cynthia Kaufman. 2012. *Getting Past Capitalism: History, Vision, Hope.* Lexington Books.
5 I first understood capitalism this way at a talk that this paper is based on: J. K. Gibson-Graham. 1993. *Waiting for the Revolution, or How to Smash Capitalism while Working at Home in Your Spare Time.* In *Rethinking Marxism,* 6.2, 10–24.
6 Peter Stearns. 2020. *Happiness in World History.* Routledge, page 89.
7 John. S. Mbiti. 1990. *African Religions and Philosophy* (2nd Edition). Heinemann, page 219.
8 Chiwoza Bandawe and Anneke Meerkotter. 2015. "Developing a conceptual framework against discrimination on the basis of gender identity." *Using the Courts to Protect Vulnerable People,* 149–161, page 152.
9 Dorine E. van Norren. 2020. "The sustainable development goals viewed through gross national happiness, Ubuntu, and Buen Vivir." *International Environmental Agreements: Politics, Law and Economics,* 20.3, 431–458.
10 Edward Skidelsky and Robert Skidelsky. 2012. *How Much Is Enough? Money and the Good Life.* Penguin, page 123.
11 Edward Diener and Eunkook M. Suh, eds. 2003. *Culture and Subjective Well-Being.* MIT Press.
12 Peter Stearns. 2020. *Happiness in World History.* Routledge, page 4.
13 Peter Stearns. 2020. *Happiness in World History.* Routledge, page 16.
14 Richard Layard. 2005. *Happiness: Lessons from a New Science.* Penguin.
15 Richard Leyte, et al. 2019. "A comparative analysis of the status anxiety hypothesis of socio-economic inequalities in health based on 18,349 individuals in four countries and five cohort studies." *Scientific Reports,* 9.1, 1–12, 2.
16 Richard Layard. 2005. *Happiness: Lessons from a New Science.* Penguin.
17 Richard Layard. 2005. *Happiness: Lessons from a New Science.* Penguin, *location 1614.*

18 Marilyn Waring. 1990. *If Women Counted: A New Feminist Economics*. Harper Collins; Kate Raworth. 2017. *Doughnut Economics: 7 Ways to Think like a 21st-Century Economist*. Chelsea Green Publishing; Juliet Shor. 1992. 2010. *Plentitude: The New Economics of True Wealth*. Penguin.

19 Joe Pinsker. 2019. "Why Are American Homes So Big?" *The Atlantic*. September 12. https://www.theatlantic.com/family/archive/2019/09/american-houses-big/597811/.

20 Fengyan Tang, et al. 2019. "The race paradox in subjective wellbeing among older Americans." *Ageing & Society*, 39.3, 568–589.

21 Fengyan Tang, et al. 2019. "The race paradox in subjective wellbeing among older Americans." *Ageing & Society,* 39.3, 568–589.

22 Tim Wadsworth and Philip Pendergast. 2021. "Race, ethnicity and subjective well-being: Exploring the disparities in life satisfaction among Whites, Latinx, and Asians." *International Journal of Wellbeing*, 11.2, 68.

23 Edward Skidelsky and Robert Skidelsky. 2012. *How Much Is Enough? Money and the Good Life*. Penguin, page 114.

24 John Iceland. 2013. *Poverty in America: A Handbook* (3rd Edition). University of California Press, page 23.

25 Quoted in Alain De Botton. 2008. *Status Anxiety*. Vintage, page 168.

26 Christoph Lakner, et al. 2019. "How Much Does Reducing Inequality Matter for Global Poverty," World Bank Working Paper 8869, page 1.

27 Anna Ratcliff. 2020. "World's Billionaires Have More Wealth Than 4.6 Billion People." Oxfam International. https://www.oxfam.org/en/press-releases/worlds-billionaires-have-more-wealth-46-billion-people.

28 Philip Alston. 2020. "The Parlous State of Poverty Eradication." Human Rights Council. July 2, page 19.

29 Hans-Otto Pörtner, et al. 2022. "Climate Change 2022: Impacts, Adaptation and Vulnerability." *IPCC Sixth Assessment Report*.

30 Troy Vettese and Drew Pendergrass. 2022. *Half-Earth Socialism: A Plan to Save the Future from Extinction, Climate Change and Pandemics*. Verso Books; Eric Dinerstein, et al. 2019. "A global deal for nature: guiding principles, milestones, and targets." *Science Advances*, 5.4, eaaw2869. https://www.science.org/doi/10.1126/sciadv.aaw2869.

31 Cynthia Kaufman. 2021. *The Sea is Rising and So Are We: A Climate Justice Handbook*. PM Press.

32 Bill Gates. 2021. *How to Avoid a Climate Disaster: The Solutions We Have and the Breakthroughs We Need*. Knopf; Michael Bloomberg and Carl Pope. 2017. *Climate of Hope: How Cities, Businesses, and Citizens Can Save the Planet*. St. Martin's Press.

33 Amartya Sen. 1982. *Poverty and Famines: An Essay on Entitlement and Deprivation*. Oxford University Press.

34 Catriona Mortimer-Sandilands and Bruce Erickson. 2010. *Queer Ecologies: Sex, Nature, Politics, Desire*. Indiana University Press, page 169.

35 Dan Gardner. 2010. Future Babble: Why Expert Predictions Fail – and Why We Believe Them Anyway. McClelland and Stewart, pages 247–248.

36 Paul R. Ehrlich and Anne H. Ehrlich. 2013. "Can a collapse of global civilization be avoided?" *Proceedings of the Royal Society B: Biological Sciences*, 280.1754, 20122845, 6.

37 William Rees. 2021. "A Note on Climate Change and Cultural Denial." https://populationmatters.org/news/2021/11/bill-rees-note-climate-change-and-cultural-denial.

38 William Rees. 2021. "A Note on Climate Change and Cultural Denial." https://populationmatters.org/news/2021/11/bill-rees-note-climate-change-and-cultural-denial.

39 M.K. Seibert and W.E. Rees. 2021. "Through the Eye of a Needle: An Eco-Heterodox Perspective on the Renewable Energy Transition," v14, 4508, page 14.

40 M.K. Seibert and W.E. Rees. 2021. "Through the Eye of a Needle: An Eco-Heterodox Perspective on the Renewable Energy Transition," v14, 4508, page 14.

41 M.K. Seibert and W.E. Rees. 2021. "Through the Eye of a Needle: An Eco-Heterodox Perspective on the Renewable Energy Transition," v14, 4508, page 11.

42 George Monbiot. 2009. "Stop Blaming the Poor. It's the Wally Yachters Who Are Burning the Planet." *The Guardian*. September 28. https://www.theguardian.com/commentisfree/cif-green/2009/sep/28/population-growth-super-rich.

43 Eileen Crist, Camilo Mora, and Robert Engelman. 2017. "The interaction of human population, food production, and biodiversity protection." *Science*, 356.6335, 260–264, 4.

44 Jake Earl, Colin Hickey, and Travis N. Reider. 2017. "Fertility, immigration, and the fight against climate Change." *Bioethics*, 31.8, 582–589, 583.

45 Paul D. Hawken, ed. 2017. *Drawdown: The Most Comprehensive Plan Ever Proposed to Reverse Global Warming*. Penguin, page 78.

46 Eileen Crist, Camilo Mora, and Robert Engelman. 2017. "The interaction of human population, food production, and biodiversity protection." *Science*, 356.6335, 260–264, 3.

47 Vasilis Fthenakis, et al. 2022. "Comment on Seibert, MK; Rees, WE Through the Eye of a Needle: An Eco-Heterodox Perspective on the Renewable Energy Transition. Energies 2021, 14, 4508." *Energies*, 15.3, 971, 11.

48 Vasilis Fthenakis, et al. 2022. "Comment on Seibert, MK; Rees, WE Through the Eye of a Needle: An Eco-Heterodox Perspective on the Renewable Energy Transition. Energies 2021, 14, 4508." *Energies*, 15.3, 971, 11.

49 Mark Jacobson. https://web.stanford.edu/group/efmh/jacobson/.

50 Georgina Gustin. 2017. "25 Fossil Fuel Producers Responsible for Half Global Emissions in Past 3 Decades." July 9, *Inside Climate News*.

51 Bill McKibben, Diana Nabiruma, and Omar Elmawi. 2021. "Let's Heed the UN's Dire Warning and Stop the East African Oil Pipeline now." *The Guardian*, August 17.

52 See Paul Hawken. 2017. *Drawdown: The Most Comprehensive Plan Ever Proposed to Reverse Global Warming*. Penguin; Johan Falk, Owen Gaffney, et al. 2019. *Exponential Roadmap: Scaling 30 Solutions to Halve Emissions by 2030*. Version 1.5. https://exponentialroadmap.org/wpcontent/uploads/2019/09/ExponentialRoadmap_1.5_20190919_Single-Pages.pdf.

53 Tim Dickinson. 2019. "Study: U.S. Fossil Fuel Subsidies Exceed Pentagon Spending." *Rolling Stone*, May 8. https://www.rollingstone.com/politics/politics-news/fossil-fuel-subsidies-pentagon-spending-imf-report-833035/. The *Rolling Stone* article relies on a study done by the International Monetary Fund: https://www.imf.org/external/pubs/ft/wp/2015/wp15105.pdf.

Chapter 2

The Psychology of Enough

When will I ever feel like I have enough? I have a nice house, a car, plenty of food, access to healthcare. And yet I still always feel like what I have seems shabby after a little while, that if I just worked a little bit harder and bought nicer things, I would be just that much happier. But really, I'm tired.[1]

Enough? I'd like to have enough. Enough to eat, a place to live, health care. Enough. What a beautiful idea.

Enough! Enough already. I have had enough of the destruction of the atmosphere, the devastation of other species, enough of letting corporations destroy the atmosphere. Enough of a world that can't even come together in a fair way to minimize deaths from a virus, that can't move fast enough to keep the planet habitable. Enough.

People want to feel good and feel good about themselves. In every society, there are ways of being that create desires and create ways to satisfy those desires. Some societies are organized such that everyone can find a place of success, and they are organized such that what leads to success for an individual will also be good for the society as a whole. In others, the balance between individual and society is structured in ways that what individuals do to be successful hurts the group as a whole. Capitalist modernity is a good example of the latter. Our social system encourages us to want more than the next person and to step onto a hedonic escalator of increasing levels of consumption. This chapter looks at what drives a culture of insatiability, what drives people to want things that are bad for society as a whole, and what we can do to disrupt those drivers, in order to build a world where everyone has enough.

Most People Like Nice Stuff

My mother was an artist and I grew up in a household without a lot of money but with a commitment to my mother's view of good taste. I grew up with a negative view of ostentation and garishness, but a deep appreciation for the

DOI: 10.4324/9781003354871-3

The Psychology of Enough   25

well-crafted, well-designed, and aesthetically pleasing. So, like many people on the planet, I have my own version of consumer pleasures. I often get homemade pottery as presents. I love my thrift store furniture. I love my high functioning garlic press and salad spinner. So, there is a piece of me that is a big-time consumer, and it is hard for me, who has enough money to buy the beautiful things I want, to say that people should do without.

In his book *Consumerism in World History*, Peter Stearns argues that what we call consumerism is something that developed in Europe at the beginning of the industrial revolution, spread to the US, and has since become as a dominant way of life in much of the world. For him, it is natural that people want nice things. But, he argues, in earlier times there were countervailing social pressures that kept those desires for nice things from having much social impact.

Before the period of the agricultural revolution, human beings lived in small relatively egalitarian bands, and many anthropologists believe that life was fairly easy in much of the world. Those societies had fairly simple levels of material wealth, and most things used were made within a group. Those societies were not impacted by the modern problems associated with consumerism.[2]

Ever since settled life and agriculture developed, human societies have struggled with high levels of inequality and with persistent problems of poverty. In the period after the agricultural revolution and before the industrial revolution, there were relatively low levels of material goods, life was hard in many places, and there wasn't enough extra to spend on things that weren't needed. Most people were not involved in what we would call consumer behavior. In pre-industrial Europe, lower class people were sanctioned if they took on the airs of higher classes. At many times and in many places, in that period, luxury was being seen as in contrast to a spiritual life.

Stearns argues that consumerism takes off when people have enough of their basic needs met that they have some disposable income, when the ideological or spiritual context doesn't prohibit it, when there is enough social mobility that status lines are not completely fixed, and when it is in the interest of some to profit on the consumer behavior of others. These are the elements that led to the origins of consumerism in Europe, which was then taken up in the US. For many years, the US has been at the forefront of the spread of a consumer lifestyle. Now, that model of living has spread through much of the world as the ideal of the good life, even in places where there is not very much material wealth.

In the period of human existence that comes after the agricultural revolution, but before the industrial revolution, in so-called preindustrial societies, there were many pleasures in everyday living that industrialism took away. In many preindustrial societies, people have had time to make nice things, share meals with others, etc. Stearns argues that in the early days of the industrial revolution in Britain, many working-class people found industrial labor miserable and found compensation in smoking cigarettes, buying something beautiful to wear, eating out at the pub or in restaurants.

Once consumerism takes off as a form of life, it comes to create whole systems of meaning and desire. Stearns argues that some of the drivers of consumerism have to do with the motive of some to profit off its promotion and from the simple fact that it gives us things we find pleasurable. But, he argues, it

> also exists because it meets other needs. Its role in responding to blurring of identity is crucial. Consumerism helps people deal with confusions about social status and with challenges to established patterns because of new foreign influence. Consumerism also relatedly, allows quiet challenges to hierarchy, in terms of social class, gender, even parental authority. It provides some sense of freedom and individual expression, however superficial the outcome. And particularly outside the West, it offers a sense of belonging to a larger whole, of gaining access to the up-to-date and modern .... People come to grow up with consumerism from infancy; they assume its logic and normalcy. The combination of three components—manipulation, fulfillment of social and personal needs, and habituation—serves as consumerism's incubator and ongoing support.[3]

For Stearns, consumerism is driven by advertising and other forms of manipulation. It is driven by a form of compensation for a life of alienated labor and overwork. And, over time, it becomes a cultural norm. Wanting nice and useful things doesn't require an explanation. What needs investigation is how we can get a world where those desires don't destroy the environment, while leaving many people unsatisfied, and others in poverty. As we think about a world of enough it is important to not minimize the real pleasures that come from consumerism. But it is also important that we take seriously how we allocate social resources and figure out ways to ensure that we don't make ourselves miserable trying make ourselves happy.

Smart for One and Dumb for All

In *Luxury Fever: Why Money Fails to Satisfy*, Robert H. Frank argues that in highly unequal consumerist societies, many people are driven to conspicuous consumption because it benefits the individual in terms of status, even though it is bad for society. It is, he claims, "smart for one and dumb for all." As we saw in Chapter 1, in a stratified society an individual is made happier by having more than others, but having more inequality in a society leads to less overall happiness. Buying consumer goods gives a short-term good feeling, but the pleasure one gets from buying things wears off quickly.[4] So, we could see the conspicuous consumption of things like larger homes, more luxury cars, and large television sets as a waste of money. But it turns out that those goods do deliver status. And higher status really does lead to higher relative happiness.[5]

Societies like the US, where there is a virtual arms race for status goods, are living out that nightmare of being driven by the status desires of people who feel a need to keep up, while neglecting to invest in the things that would make everyone better off. Frank argues that there are policies that can keep these sorts of arms races from taking off. To illustrate this point, he gives the example of a town along a strip of highway with no regulations on signs. Every business will compete to have larger and more garish signs to attract more customers. But if the town were to enact a law that limited the size of signs, then everyone, would be better off. The town looks better, and the store owners are not compelled to waste money on huge signs.[6] The big signs are "smart for one but dumb for all."

Frank's main solution to the problem of wasting money as a society on conspicuous consumption is to enact a steep consumption tax. If very rich people aren't pulling us upward in our sense of status by their consumption choices, then we will not feel compelled as a society to waste money on status items. Chapter 7 will explore this and many other policy choices that can decrease status anxiety, increase a sense of belonging, and lead to higher levels of social solidarity and happiness.

Stories of Success

Human societies generally have stories people tell about what it means to be a good person. People are judged, and judge themselves, on the basis of those stories. There have been plenty of societies in human history that haven't had status anxiety as a problem. If you were a serf in medieval Europe, you probably didn't feel ashamed that you were a common person, because that wasn't seen by yourself, or anyone else, as your fault. Generally, in societies with social stability, one might be materially deprived by having a low socioeconomic status, but worry about status would probably not be a big part of one's inner life.

Any society that has pathways open for people to change their status, and where being considered a good person is contingent on something that one can worry about losing, is going to be a society that generates status anxiety. The history of literature is full of stories of great warriors, rulers, and adventurers, who sought to attain something great, or great anti-heroes who are driven by avarice and an insatiable need for glory. In both cases we watch with fascination and empathy, or disgust and horror, as they face the challenges to achieve their goals. These stories still resonate with us because there's something we can relate to in a person trying to be great and facing all of the traps that can lead to shame and failure.

28 The Psychology of Enough

Heroic epics tend to come out of highly stratified societies, such as ancient Egypt, Sumer, China, India, Japan, and medieval Europe. Generally, heroic stories are set in times of warfare, when there is social instability. The hero is an extraordinary individual, and usually someone from an elite background, but whose status is unstable. In the societies which form the backdrop of these epic legends, there are lots of regular people living regular lives, not wrapped up in the search for glory. For those people, status is fairly stable.

Many societies throughout history have had a class of people who were driven by a desire for wealth for its own sake. In his play, *Wealth,* Aristophanes writes, "If a man has eighty thousand drachmas, he's all the more set on getting a hundred thousand; and once he's got that, he says life's not worth living unless he makes a quarter of a million."[7] The ancient Greek legend of King Midas tells of a person who loves gold so much that he thinks it is a great idea to make everything touches turn into gold, until he realizes that this makes him unable to eat. These stories tell us two things, that an insatiable desire for wealth is old and that there have been storytellers for a long time warning us against the dangers of avarice. It seems that as long as there is a possibility of increasing status through wealth, some people will want to gain extraordinary wealth and will want the trappings that signal wealth to others.

Both Aristophanes' play and the ancient Greek story of King Midas are cautionary tales to warn us against avarice. In order to keep what is smart for one from causing social outcomes that are dumb for all, many societies have had mechanisms in place to limit avarice. These stories that warn us against avarice exist, in part, to keep us from making the mistake of greed. Many small-scale indigenous societies have stronger mechanisms to prevent "good for one dumb for all" from emerging. One well-known example is the system of potlatch in the Pacific Northwest of the US and Canada. In this system, wealthy and politically powerful people would show their status by giving away or destroying the things that have given them wealth and status.

In his book *Status Anxiety,* Alan de Botton argues that in the Western world for two millennia there were three main stories people told about wealth and poverty, which made it not shameful to be poor. One was the medieval view that peasants provided for the basic needs of society and thus, it was honorable to be poor. The second was a Christian notion that all are beloved by God and that poverty is neither shameful nor honorable. The third story was developed by thinkers such as Rousseau and Marx, and it claimed that the wealthy gained their riches through exploitation and robbery, and thus it was immoral to be wealthy.

This set of stories began to be replaced in the period of the industrial revolution. The new stories made the case that the rich are the ones responsible for creating wealth; that wealth is a sign that one is favored by God; and finally, that society is a meritocracy, so one's wealth or poverty is a result of one's own virtue or lack of virtue.[8] All six of these stories are with us in the present moment. de Botton argues that the latter set of stories has been more impactful in recent decades and have set us up for deep feelings of status anxiety, as our success as a person, whether we are seen as good or bad by others, becomes infected with beliefs that being wealthy and showing wealth are virtues.

In the US, the rhetoric of meritocracy has been used in especially devastating ways to blame Black people for their poverty. After the urban uprisings of the late 1960s, many policy makers in the US looked to see how future unrest could be prevented. In 1967 President Johnson pulled together a commission headed by Illinois Governor Otto Kerner to investigate their causes. The Kerner Commission found that lack of opportunity, police brutality, a hostile media, and poor social services were the root causes of Black poverty. The report was published in a book form and was a nationwide best seller. In spite of that analysis, few of the recommendations of the report were acted on.

A different narrative of the causes of the unrest developed at the same time. In 1965 Daniel Patrick Moynihan, who would go on to have a long career as a liberal in the Senate, published the book *The Negro Family*, which argued that the roots of Black poverty lay in the structure of the Black family. His theory came to be known as the "culture of poverty." It argued that Black people had little drive, ambition, or work ethic, and their families were structured in ways that did not promote healthy character development. That view, held by liberals as well as conservatives, has become widely accepted in the culture as a commonsense truth. Black people need to do something differently if they want not to be poor. The view that Black poverty is caused by something carried by Black people themselves then leads well-meaning policy makers to focus antipoverty efforts on teaching financial literacy, job readiness, and parenting skills.

And yet, as William A. Darity, Jr. and A. Kirsten Mullen argue in *From Here to Equality: Reparations for Black Americans in the Twenty-First Century*, "the black savings rate is comparable to the white savings rate at each level of household income."[9] "For comparable levels of family socioeconomic status, black youth obtain more years of schooling and credentials, including college degrees, than white youth."[10] They argue that historic differences in access to wealth via inheritance from parents and grandparents, as well as access to quality loans to buy homes, account for differences in wealth. "Blacks, whose incomes were about $60,000 in 2014 had a level of median wealth of about $22,000, while whites whose incomes were less than $26,000 had a median wealth of about $18,000."[11]

Blacks are attaining degrees and saving money at the same levels of whites at comparable wealth levels. The structural forces of redlining and discrimination from banks, and discriminatory government programs, have denied Black people in the US the ability to buy homes in places that will hold value. The main driver in difference in levels of attainment is difference in access to wealth. Black people are on average more poor than white people because they lack access to money, not because they don't strive.

It is bad enough to be poor, but it is devastating to be gaslit everyday by living in a society that says that your poverty is your fault or the fault of your family. In my work with low-income students of color at De Anza College, I find that teaching about systems of domination has a powerful psychological effect on my students, as they come to see that the struggles they experience in life are not primarily the result of something wrong with themselves or their families. Developing critical consciousness about the world around them helps them to see themselves as wrapped up in larger historical processes, which they can have an impact on changing as they look outward at the causes of the misery in their lives, as opposed to internalizing feelings of shame along with a lack of material resources.

There are economic processes which leave huge parts of the planet deprived of investment capital, which allocate resources based on money and allow those with a lot to pass a lot on to their children, which give wildly different access to education to people of different classes and races. In the current world, almost everywhere, there is deep shame in poverty. Our world is significantly less meritocratic than dominant narratives would have. The socially corrosive belief that society places people in a hierarchy based on their talent and drive is widespread. False belief in meritocracy leads to a misdiagnosis of our social problems. It leads our attention away from otherwise obvious solutions to the problem of poverty, such as giving resources to the poor and stopping discriminatory lending practices. It is psychologically devastating to people who are blamed for their own poverty. It also encourages the wealthy to overestimate their own virtues, while discouraging them from having empathy for others.

There is something really peculiar and destructive about how status anxiety manifests in modern capitalist society, where everyone is judged based on a set of standards that are virtually unattainable. Even the people at the top worry about their place in the Forbes magazine list of the wealthiest people. And all the rest of us struggle to find ways to feel good about ourselves in a world constantly telling us we need to buy more, and present ourselves in status seeking ways, to be acceptable.

Many societies in human history have had mechanisms, both material and ideological, for limiting the impacts of avarice on society. Societies that take avarice as a social good are historically rare. Spreading the view that greed is good for society, and undermining traditional limits to avarice, took a lot of intellectual work over the past several centuries by pro-capitalist thinkers. It may be that it is "natural" for people to want to be better than their neighbors and to find their sense of well-being by having more than them, but society doesn't have to be run in ways that promote that antisocial behavior. Rather, part of building a good society is finding ways to limit the impacts of avarice on our social decision-making processes.

A drive for status based on wealth is not new with capitalism, but capitalism is unparalleled in doing several things that make status anxiety into a society wide problem. First, it bases our social standing on things we need to compete for, while making to access to the things needed to live on precarious. Second, it perpetuates narratives that successful people are those who engage in more conspicuous consumption. Third, it argues that people who have less wealth contribute less to society and have themselves to blame for their poverty. Finally, once a society has a high level of stratification, those with more power are able to impose the rules and system of ideas under which that society operates on others and can turn inequality into greater, and ever more justified, inequality.

Relative poverty is created by a mismatch between what a person is expected to have in a given society and what they have access to. Status anxiety is created by a society making it difficult, or impossible, to have what one needs to have in order to be considered in a positive way by one's peers. It can be contingent on things one can't control, like the race or class, or where one is born. Or it can be contingent on the things one strives for such as prestigious jobs, consumer goods, or demonstrations of "good taste."

The Biology of Status Anxiety

We can learn some things about status anxiety by looking at its impacts on the body. Social scientists have discovered that there is a protein in our bodies, C-reactive protein (CRP) that indicates our levels of stress and trauma. Richard Layte and his co-authors studied the relationship between CRP, socioeconomic position (SEP), and a nation's inequality in Europe. After controlling for other health factors, what they found was that

> *Everyone* experiences higher psycho-social stress and inflammatory response in more unequal societies, not just those in the lowest SEP. The extent of perceived *status anxiety* has been shown to vary significantly across European countries by SEP and more unequal countries (as measured by income inequality) have larger differentials in perceived status anxiety by SEP and worse mental health. Moreover, more unequal countries have higher status anxiety overall. The highest SEP groups in more unequal societies have similar levels of status anxiety to the lowest SEP groups in more equal societies.[12]

High levels of inequality in a society that values wealth as a sign of success cause psychological and physical harm to everyone. Inequality causes stress even for the wealthy, even while it causes more stress for people at the lower levels of society.

Meaning and Inequality

In 1930 John Maynard Keynes published an essay "Economic Possibilities for our Grandchildren," which argued that human society was on a path to a situation where people's basic needs would soon easily be met. But, he saw a new set of problems emerging over that horizon. He saw a glimpse of that future in the empty and unsatisfying lives of pleasure and status seeking in the lives of the wealthy. Human beings needed to get to work developing ways to have meaning and joy in life from things other than status-driven consumption.

He wrote,

> There are no country and no people, I think, who can look forward to the age of leisure and of abundance without a dread. For we have been trained too long to strive and not to enjoy. It is a fearful problem for the ordinary person, with no special talents, to occupy himself, especially if he no longer has roots in the soil or in custom or in the beloved conventions of a traditional society. To judge from the behaviour and the achievements of the wealthy classes to-day in any quarter of the world, the outlook is very depressing! For these are, so to speak, our advance guard-those who are spying out the promised land for the rest of us and pitching their camp there. For they have most of them failed disastrously, so it seems to me-those who have an independent income but no associations or duties or ties-to solve the problem which has been set them.[13]

In his book *Affluence without Abundance: The Disappearing World of the Bushmen*, anthropologist James Suzman argues that inequality makes it very difficult for people to live lives full of meaning and connection. The book is based on work he did among the Omaheke Ju/'hosani people of Namibia. These are people who have been deprived of the best land they used to live on, and so are now some of the poorest people on the planet, both in terms of how much they consume and in terms of health and well-being. His study examines the worldview of the older society that he still saw remnants of. He argued that even with a relatively low level of material abundance, before their forms of life were destroyed by dispossession, these people felt like they had enough. They saw themselves as affluent.

These people had a form of life that had its own challenges, and forms of status and interpersonal conflict. But it also had enough rich connections to allow people to feel that theirs was a good life. Suzman writes that if we are wanting to find lives where we feel that we have enough, we need to deal with the problem of inequality:

> For the hunter-gatherer model of primitive affluence as not simply based on their having few needs easily satisfied; it also depended on

no one being substantially richer or more powerful than anyone else. If this kind of egalitarianism is a precondition for us to embrace a post-labor world, then I suspect it may prove to be a very hard nut to crack.[14]

Solutions to the Problem of Status Anxiety

People who live in societies with high levels of inequality will always find it very difficult to live happy lives and to ever feel that they have enough. The most important step to building a world of enough is to challenge inequality. In *The Spirit Level: Why Great Equality Makes Societies Stronger*, Kate Pickett and Richard Wilkinson make a very compelling case, backed by significant empirical evidence, that economic inequality is a primary driver of many forms of social dysfunction.[15] They argue that on many measures of social well-being, societies with higher levels of inequality have worse social outcomes. While race and gender are significant aspects of inequality, Pickett and Wilkinson focus mostly on economic inequality.

Their examples of the forms of social dysfunction that are positively correlated with inequality include mental health, incarceration rates, mortality, educational attainment, teen pregnancy, lower levels of social mobility, and more. And one interesting finding is that in all of these examples, the negative impacts are not just for the poor or for the society on average. The well off in unequal countries also do worse on these measures as well.

They argue that there is a

> tendency for some countries to do well on just about everything and others to do badly. You can predict a countries' performance on one outcome from a knowledge of others. If—for instance—a country does badly on health, you can predict with some confidence that it will also imprison a larger proportion of its population, have more teenage pregnancies, lower literacy scores, more obesity, worse mental health, and so on. Inequality seems to make countries socially dysfunctional across a wide range of outcomes.[16]

They write that in contemporary societies with high levels of inequality, people have become

> highly self-conscious, obsessed with how we appear to others, worried that we might come across as unattractive, boring, stupid, or whatever, and constantly trying to manage the impressions we make. And at the core of our interactions with strangers is our concern at the social judgements and evaluations they may make: how do they rate us, did we give

34 The Psychology of Enough

a good account of ourselves? This vulnerability is part of the modern psychological condition that feeds directly into consumerism.

... Greater inequality seems to heighten people's social evaluation anxieties by increasing importance of social status. Instead of accepting each other as equals on the basis of our common humanity as we might in more equal settings, getting the measure of each other becomes more important as status differences widen. We come to see social position as a more important feature of a person's identity.[17]

Citing Oliver James' book *Affluenza*, they argue that more unequal societies tend to place

a high value on acquiring money and possessions, looking good in the eyes of others and wanting to be famous. These kinds of values place us at greater risk of depression, anxiety, substance abuse, and personality disorder.[18]

One conclusion that they draw from this research is that, for a country with high levels of inequality, work done to fight for more positive outcomes for the poor in terms of education or health outcomes, for example, treat the symptoms rather that the roots of the disease, and only marginal success can be made.

Pickett and Wilkinson also argue that once a society has a high level of inequality, levels of trust deteriorate, and that leads to more mistrust, which then leads to support for policies that lead to more inequality. "Mistrust and inequality reinforce each other."[19] The politics fanning the flames of ethno-nationalism and racism that we see accelerating in many countries around the world are in part a result of politicians exploiting the lack of social solidarity that comes from life in an unequal society. And as people come to feel insecure, and vote based on fear, and as politicians are then able to stoke hatred of others based on those fears, it is a short step to the anti-democratic and authoritarian politics that have been emerging in many countries in recent years. Fighting against inequality is one of the most urgent goals of the present period. Significant and lasting social improvements happen when societies take action to reduce inequality. Ways to fight inequality, and to build a politics based on solidarity, are subjects we will return to in Chapter 7.

A few lessons from this:

1 Policies that lead to higher levels of equality are likely to lead to higher levels of happiness. Extreme wealth taxes are good for everyone, even those at the top. As long as his mansion is the biggest, it doesn't matter to the ultra-wealthy of the world how big their mansion actually is.

2 We need to elevate stories which give realistic views of why some people have more than others and bring back the stories that help explain and generate empathy for those who our social systems deprive of the resources necessary to live well.
3 There is cultural work to be done to make being a luxury consumer into something that is socially stigmatized.

It is almost impossible for individuals to fight the pull of destructive forms of status without real policy changes that decrease inequality.

Notes

1 These statements, when they don't have a separate footnote, are made up and are intended to represent the kinds of things people say on the subject of the chapter.
2 Peter N. Stearns. 2020. *Happiness in World History*. Routledge. Chapter 1. The book that did the most to promote this view of pre-agricultural well-being was Marshal Sahlins. 1972. *Stone Age Economics*. de Gruyter.
3 Peter N. Stearns. 2006. *Consumerism in World History: The Global Transformation of Desire*. Routledge, pages 153–154.
4 Robert H. Frank. 2001. *Luxury Fever: Why Money Fails to Satisfy in an Era of Excess*. Simon and Schuster, page 179.
5 Robert H. Frank. 2001. *Luxury Fever: Why Money Fails to Satisfy in an Era of Excess*. Simon and Schuster, page 137.
6 Robert H. Frank. 2001. *Luxury Fever: Why Money Fails to Satisfy in an Era of Excess*. Simon and Schuster, page 166.
7 Edward Skidelsky and Robert Skidelsky. 2012. *How Much Is Enough? Money and the Good Life*. Penguin, page 76.
8 Alan de Botton. 2008. *Status Anxiety*. Vintage, page 55.
9 William A. Darity Jr and A. Kirsten Mullen. 2020. *From Here to Equality: Reparations for Black Americans in the Twenty-first Century*. UNC Press Books, page 46.
10 William A. Darity Jr and A. Kirsten Mullen. 2020. *From Here to Equality: Reparations for Black Americans in the Twenty-first Century*. UNC Press Books, page 47.
11 William A. Darity Jr and A. Kirsten Mullen. 2020. *From Here to Equality: Reparations for Black Americans in the Twenty-first Century*. UNC Press Books, page 47.
12 Richard Layte, et al. 2019. "A comparative analysis of the status anxiety hypothesis of socio-economic inequalities in health based on 18,349 individuals in four countries and five cohort studies." *Scientific Reports*, 9.1, 1–12, 2.
13 Keynes, John Maynard. 2016. "Economic Possibilities for our Grandchildren." In *Essays in Persuasion*. Springer, page 328.
14 Suzman, James. 2017. *Affluence without Abundance: The Disappearing World of the Bushmen*. Bloomsbury Publishing USA, page 256.
15 Kate Pickett and Richard Wilkinson. 2011. *The Spirit Level: Why Great Equality Makes Societies Stronger*. Bloomsbury Press.
16 Kate Pickett and Richard Wilkinson. 2011. *The Spirit Level: Why Great Equality Makes Societies Stronger*. Bloomsbury Press, page 253.
17 Kate Pickett and Richard Wilkinson. 2011. *The Spirit Level: Why Great Equality Makes Societies Stronger*. Bloomsbury Press, page 78–79.
18 Kate Pickett and Richard Wilkinson. 2011. *The Spirit Level: Why Great Equality Makes Societies Stronger*. Bloomsbury Press, page 114.
19 Kate Pickett and Richard Wilkinson. 2011. *The Spirit Level: Why Great Equality Makes Societies Stronger*. Bloomsbury Press, page 95.

Chapter 3

Building a Life with Enough

> My home is full of so much crap. I saw a beautiful magazine at my friend's house called *Simplicity*. That's how I want my house to look. Calm, well designed, serene, and simple. I want to be free of clutter and disorder. I'm going to buy a book on simplicity, and go to the organizer store. Maybe then I'll feel good.[1]

> I'm not going to buy my way to goodness. I am going to go vegan, stop flying, make my own soap and clothes, and grow vegetables. I am not responsible for other people and I can't make them change. Maybe if I do this, others will follow me. Maybe that's how we stop the madness of climate destruction. Whether or not it changes anyone else, at least I'll know I am doing the right thing.

> My life is plenty simple. Because I can't afford to buy stuff. What a funny problem, to not know where to put your third television set. I guess I am the new status symbol. Because I don't have a car. I don't fly. And I certainly don't waste money on yachts.

> All of that is so dumb. No one cares how you live. And me not flying is going to make zero difference. I am going to work on policy changes and keep eating meat and flying for as long as other people do it.

People in the US tend to assume that the solutions to problems lie with the personal choices of individuals. Generally, they see the world through lens of psychology more than sociology. The US is especially far along the historical shift that has taken place over the past hundred years, all around the world, of people primarily seeing themselves not as citizens of a nation, or of the world, but, rather, primarily as consumers. If I am a consumer, then I change the world through my consumption choices, and if the world has too much consumerism, I should consume less or consume differently. And yet, as the rest of this book argues, getting to a world of enough requires much more than a shift in personal consumption. Individual consumption shifts do not have nearly as broad an impact as changes in policies. As long as society is

DOI: 10.4324/9781003354871-4

driven by the profit motive and devastated by inequality, personal lifestyle changes are like swimming upstream in a raging river. Investigating how to make those larger social shifts happen is the work of Chapter 7.

And yet, even if I live in a raging river pushing me and all the fish around me toward consumerism and waste, I still experience my life in the small part of the river where I live and face a life full of a thousand small choices every day. Should I give that person on the street a dollar? Should I save money? Should I go back to school? Should I share my fears about the future with my family? Should I tell that person what I think? Should I polish my nails? Should I try to buy a house? Should I eat meat? Should I make myself feel happy by indulging in a small purchase? Should I fly for a vacation?

This chapter looks at some of the ways that personal lifestyle choices are wrapped up in how to get to a world of enough. Whether or not these choices make a large difference, each of us is faced with these kinds of choices every day. Individuals are part of communities. To some extent, we create and transform culture through how we live, and so we can have some small impact on our shared situation by changing how we live. And those choices can have a large impact on our own happiness. This chapter will look at some of the unhelpful ways that people focus on lifestyle choices, and it looks at some recent research on how shifts in lifestyle and consumption patterns can add up to significant differences.

Anti-consumerist Consumerism

There is a magazine called *Real Simple*. You can buy it and see beautiful pictures of homes without too much stuff in them. In them you also see an aesthetic of high quality, visually austere, things. The idea is that less is better and that we should attend to our surroundings and take away the clutter and replace it with beautiful well-designed things, so that our surroundings can help give us a sense of calm and order. Aesthetic minimalism and calm design can be an incredibly attractive antidote to lives filled with clutter and stress. During the pandemic, as many people were forced to show the insides of their homes to coworkers through their video calls, many opted instead to put on a virtual background. And many chose as backgrounds rooms with those simple, sleek, aesthetics.

It isn't helpful to challenging status-driven consumption to promote a new status symbol of living in a beautifully well-appointed home with lots of sleek and simple stuff which all cost a lot of money to buy. So many of the self-help books around happiness and decluttering and downshifting to a simpler life presume an already rich reader who is looking for simplicity. When simplicity guru Marie Kondo tells us how we can be much happier if we get rid of old clothes we never wear and organize our drawers using cardboard boxes, she is helping us increase our happiness. But as soon as decluttering becomes a reason to buy lot of plastic organizers and higher quality, simpler looking lamps, we have moved into a different form of consumerism that brings with it environmental destruction, and which generates status anxiety, instead of helping us move toward an appreciation of enough.

One of the dangers of consuming our way to simplicity is that it can become a new form of status. Doing simplicity as the magazines show probably requires a housekeeper to keep it as clean as it needs to be to look really simple. Those with the money, time, and an inclination to buy their way to this simple aesthetic are ahead in the status game from people who have crummy clunky things, and who might be too busy doing other things to make their homes look simple.

It is almost impossible for things in our society to escape being commodified. And so, even simplicity has become a commodity. Subscribe to the magazine. Buy the books. Take the workshops. Buy the organizing bins. Buy higher quality simpler stuff. But if the whole point is to get off of the consumer treadmill, for environmental reasons, and to live happier lives free of consume pressures, then this is a misplaced solution. Decluttering and simplifying can be great ways to be happier in one's situation, but a move to voluntary simplicity needs to be made with caution about engaging in new forms of status seeking consumerism.

Wealthy People Downshifting

There are many people in wealthy countries who are engaging in forms of voluntary simplicity that don't fall into this consumerist trap. Instead of buying their way to a simple life, they are simplifying by working less and buying less. They are quitting high pressure jobs and watching their budgets carefully so that they don't spend frivolously, all to free themselves from the rat race. This voluntary choice to work less, and consume less, is called "downshifting." Many downshifters are finding happiness in a simpler life that is not based on consumerism and money-based status seeking.

To engage in this lifestyle, it is important that one should not be so poor so as to need to work three jobs to support a family. But there is a class of people who do have some room for choosing between work and leisure and can make concerted choices in favor of leisure. This choice involves detaching from the pull to work longer hours in order to buy unnecessary things. These people don't go out to dinner with friends, they cook with them at home. They spend time making things and sharing things. They build community and engage in pleasures that don't involve buying and spending.

Economist Adel Daoud is interested in challenging the idea, propagated by mainstream economics, that people can never have enough. His work rejects the idea in mainstream economics that economic thinking should start from the assumption that human beings live in an inevitable state of scarcity. Instead, he argues that there are complex relationships between scarcity, abundance, and sufficiency. For him, an important part of economic thinking should be to attend to the relationships between those three states.[2] In his work on downshifters, he shows that it is possible, for people with enough resources, to escape a life lived with a feeling of scarcity and instead to lives full of abundance.

In his research on downshifters, Daoud found that the people he studied were able to find increased levels of happiness by making individual choices to consume less. One crucial ingredient he found in those who made this shift successfully was that they moved away from participating in the mainstream culture that values status-driven consumption. In his study of people who chose to step off the consumer treadmill, Daoud found that

> These simplifiers consequently manage, though with difficulty due to causal interference, to deflate their material wants and maintain them below their material means. Consequently, they actualize the modus vivendi of material simplicity; namely, a practical state of relative abundance.[3]

Daoud found that downshifters were much more likely to be successful if they had enough money to not be caught in the trap of needing a full-time job to meet their basic survival needs. That, of course, it is much easier if one is in a country that doesn't require a full-time job for decent medical care. But with those caveats, Daoud is making an important point. It is possible for some people to resist the pulls of consumerism by intentionally choosing to do so and to live lives where they feel a sense of abundance.

There are people promoting downshifting, and taking it to a new level by encouraging others to retire at a young age. They call their movement FIRE: Financial Independence Retire Early. If you get a professional job, and continue to live as you did before you got that job, and save half your salary, many people with average professional level jobs in the wealthy countries of the global north can retire in early middle age.

Some of the literature from this movement is horribly classist and claims that everyone should do it. But, of course, most people in most countries of the world are just getting by and the pleasure of an occasional meal out is a significant form of relief from a life of hard work. And for most people simply choosing to not spend frivolously isn't enough to escape the trap of working for a wage. And yet in spite of its classist blind spots, the people who are doing this are showing something worth looking at. They highlight the reality that is often hidden for many people that there are tradeoffs that sometimes can be made between working and consuming, and that for many people the drive for a bigger car, bigger house, or status vacations, in fact, do trap them into a cycle of more work and less joy. There are quite a few people for whom there is a larger margin for choice than they might think in choosing between work and leisure, between status in the mainstream and higher levels of happiness.

40 Building a Life with Enough

While some individuals can make some choices to downshift, this is an area where policy changes can make individual choices much easier. Where there is a minimum wage high enough to support living on one job, working less is easier. Where health care and old age care are available, separately from a job, working less is easier. Where there is support for parents taking time off to care for young children, and college education is free, it is easier for people to choose to work less. How to make these changes happen is explored in Chapter 7.

Subcultures of Consumption

It is a well-established pattern that as people gain higher incomes, they generally also move into higher consumption social circles, and so they feel just as needy and unsatisfied, and just as worried about money, as they did before. It takes real conscious effort to not be on the hedonic escalator that drives us toward wanting more and never being happy with what we have.

As we saw above, some people who have enough money to move into a higher consumption bracket chose instead to restrict their spending. They enact moratoriums on buying new clothes, or new anything, learn to fix things, and find pleasure in enough. And they spread that set of values and way of living through friends and co-workers. They do that by not going on carbon emitting vacations and bragging about them; by not remodeling their home and bragging about it; by finding other things to show pride in and to complement in others. As individuals we can live differently and spread values that support living with enough.

Many people know that life is about more than simple individualistic pleasure and status seeking. For many people, alternatives to consumerist culture have a spiritual cast to them. Buddhist monks, and monks of many kinds, have found well-being in simple lives at low levels of consumption. Many movements for voluntary simplicity, such as the Amish and Mennonites, have as part of their spiritual practice renouncing the lures of consumer culture. And yet many of those subcultures have built into in them aesthetic approaches to life that are anti-pleasure, which limit their appeal.

Some of the liberation movements of the twentieth century, such as the queer liberation movement and women's movement, have taken the right to bodily pleasure to be important aspects of liberation. In her book *Pleasure Activism*, Adriene Maree Brown argues that a significant part of liberation is for oppressed people to prioritize their own pleasure:

> Part of the reason so few of us have a healthy relationship with pleasure is because a small minority of our species hoards the excess of resources, creating false scarcity and then trying to sell us joy, sell us back to ourselves. ... A central aspect of pleasure activism is tapping into the natural abundance that exists within and between our species and the planet.

Pleasure is not one of the spoils of capitalism. It is what our bodies, our human system are structured for.[4]

We should be able to find our way to lives filled with joy, pleasure, and meaning, without succumbing to consumerism. One way to do that is to live in subcultures where the systems of meaning support our choices to consume less, where among one's friends and loved ones, we share a rejection of dominant systems of meaning and where our chosen ways of living are reflected and supported. And yet, as anyone trying to raise an anti-consumerist child within mainstream culture knows, those living in subcultures resistant to consumerism always need to navigate the intersections of their subculture and the dominant one, and that involves inevitable compromise and tension.

In *Luxury Fever*, Frank tells an interesting story about himself that raises the question of subcultures. Once, a family member needed to get rid of a Porsche at a very low price and, as a car lover, he thought of buying it. But he was living in Ithaca, New York at the time, a liberal college town with a culture that ran counter to conspicuous consumption. He decided not to buy the car even though he wanted it, because he thought it would negatively impact his social status.[5]

His story makes a crucial point: culture matters. When we look for status, we look for it within the culture that matters to us. In the subcultures where I mostly get my sense of status, doing social change work is better for gaining status than buying a $50,000 watch. In my world, no one would know the value of that watch and if they did, they would think there was something wrong with me for buying one.

During World War II when many individuals in countries fighting against fascism were united in helping support the war effort, wearing a fur coat was considered antisocial behavior. If you had that much money, it was thought that you should spend it on the war effort, and not on things that made other people feel badly about their own poverty. That new imperative spread culture wide and for a short period had huge impacts.

As long as we live in a society that values conspicuous consumption as a path to status, the work of individuals to resist those pulls will not be enough to transform society toward healthy spending patterns. An important part of getting to a world of enough is the cultural work we do to transform the narratives that circulate in society. Some people do that with art work, writing, making movies, creating memes. Most of us also participate in that cultural work of supporting and undermining dominant narratives with the stories we tell ourselves and others, with what we chose to post on social media, in how we tell our stories to others.

I have wondered recently if part of the increasing appeal in recent years of super hero movies is related to a search for narratives of success that are more compelling than the insatiable drive to have a nicer kitchen than one's neighbors. The heroes in superhero movies are almost always trying to achieve something worthwhile, like saving a nation or the planet, or some vulnerable people. Perhaps we are coming at a time of shifting culture where the consumerist illusion is beginning to be tarnished, as it is increasingly linked with environmental catastrophe and lives lacking meaning or community.

In the early phase of the COVID-19 crisis there was a momentary shift in dominant narratives about who are successful people. The heroes for a few months were the janitors who risked their lives to clean the New York City subways, the healthcare workers who risked their lives to save others, and the public health officials who used their scientific knowledge to develop the policies needed to keep us safe. The crisis made it manifestly clear that farmworkers are more important than investment bankers. For a moment many people could see the matrix of our shared lives. For a few short months, many people were commenting on how odd it was to idolize celebrities who entertain us, or billionaires who rob us of our shared wealth, while ignoring the people who actually feed us and protect our health.

Spreading Cultures of Less Consumption

My mother grew up poor, in the servant class in Greenwich, Connecticut, the town where I was born to 20-year-old white parents. Greenwich is the wealthiest town in the US. As a result of her background, my mother never wanted her children to look messy or ragged. When we moved to California in 1967, and as being disheveled became a fashion, I had quite a few fights with my mother about the state of my hair. While I didn't have enough money spent on my clothes for me to be in the higher status set in school, unlike my mother, I grew up with enough wealth and white privilege, to not feel a need to worry about looking poor.

One of the things that makes escaping the status treadmill hard is the judgment of others. If you are a person who has some trauma from being mistreated because you grew up poor, then this path is not likely to be attractive. While people in the middle of the economic strata can easily risk a sense of being an outsider and some small shame at not keeping up, if they chose to not compete in the world of status, those who have lived further down the status ladder, risk being thrown into a deep form of shame if they don't keep up. If you grew up with kids making fun of you in school because your clothes were old and had stains and holes, or if your teeth look bad because you can't afford dental work, then wearing old clothes because you don't feel like working a lot of hours to buy newer ones isn't likely to be an attractive option. Or if it is, it requires a lot of more mental landmines to be navigated than it does for someone who does not carry trauma around class or race.

Downshifters can be helpful to building a world of enough if they use their time off to advocate for policy changes that makes downshifting easier for others. If they want to be helpful in moving us toward a world of enough, they need to be careful of being judgmental of others for whom downshifting is not a choice that can be made without real hard costs. While it is a good thing to consume less, it is also not helpful to be judgmental of others who don't have the psychological or material privilege to downshift. It is also a good idea for a downshifter to look at themselves before looking to judge others. I have seen many people who downshift on one place being highly judgmental of others who are wasteful in ways different from themselves. The stereotypical example of this are environmentalists who are very hostile to people who drive gas guzzling cars, but who fly regularly for environmentally themed vacations.

Generating systems of meaning that favor less wasteful lifestyles is important for building a world of enough. Large-scale and significant changes often do come as a result of cultural movements. Vegetarianism and veganism are a good example. For many years, there has been a subset of the population which doesn't eat meat or doesn't eat animal products. People do this for a variety of reasons. For some it is about health, for some animal welfare, for some it is a spiritual choice, for others it is about the environment. As a result of their way of living, there is a wide body of knowledge about ways to eat well without animal products and several different subcultures of aesthetics around it. Now, as the environmental argument for not consuming animal products is becoming very strong, that early work makes it much easier for new people to hop on that bandwagon and eat well without consuming animal products. People who don't eat meat are not going to support government subsidies for meat production, and they are going to spread to others who they know practice of eating well without eating meat.

Similarly, in many countries in the global north, young people are questioning car-centered culture. Many are learning to drive late or not at all, and many see cars as a negative part of our societies and see driving as antisocial behavior. As fewer of them drive, more of them put pressure on our systems to provide good public transportation. Cars are one of the most important status symbols in the US. And people often spend more than they need to get a car that has the cache and image they want to project to the world. And yet, increasingly, for many young people, not owning a car is a cooler, and hence a higher status, choice.

Significant social change can happen through the spread of these kinds of cultural movements. But it is also important if you want to intentionally spread an individual practice, you need to think about what will make it attractive to other people. If being a vegan makes you a good person, and all other people are bad people, and you communicate that strongly, people are likely to develop defenses against your arguments for veganism. Part of spreading an ethical lifestyle needs to be making that lifestyle seem attractive.

We all make some choices about how we want to live and what makes us feel good. Individual downshifting can be counterproductive if the downshifter comes to be seen as a terrible kind of person, who shames others and perpetuates the spread of new forms of status anxiety. Most people don't want to sacrifice or be seen as outsiders. If environmentalist lifestyles are seen as a sacrifice that morally righteous people take, they will remain a niche phenomenon, and those sacrifices may actually slow the spread of ideas of sufficiency. An important part of work to spread the kind of cultures that allow us to feel good without wasting resources, and perpetuating toxic patterns of status seeking, is to make them look appealing.

There is no getting around the fact that people are driven to seek pleasure and that they want good social standing among others. Lives of simplicity can be lived with grace and pleasure. They will only spread if they can be made to seem attractive, desirable, and signs, to the people we look to for our status cues, that we are successful. And still, all of those changes will be uphill battles for as long as we live in a society based on people gaining wealth in ways that make others feel insecure. There are social drivers of the current path toward disaster, and we need to work on shifting those drivers. Chapter 7 focuses on the larger scale policy changes that will make it easier to live an individual life focused on enough.

Living Joyfully in Our Bodies

One of the hardest places to develop a positive aesthetics of enough is in our relationship to our own body and appearance. Feeling a need to be physically attractive is probably a human universal. And yet different societies have different standards and ways of achieving those standards. For those of us living in capitalist modernity, especially for women, it is almost impossible to simply be happy with a well-functioning body. Many people as they age, and begin to experience failures in the functioning of the body, come to realize how little they appreciated the joys of feet and legs that worked, and what a waste it was to spend years fretting about the ways those feet and legs didn't conform to some standard of beauty they didn't attain.

There are ways as individuals we can work to allow ourselves to feel joy in living the bodies we have. But in a society obsessed with youthful beauty and with very narrow range of physical types which are marked as beautiful at any given point in time, it is very difficult to simply feel good in our bodies. There are studies which show that the more advertisements we look at, the more we despise our own bodies.[5] People are either more or less attracted to us, not just as lovers, but as human beings, based on a whole range of more and less acceptable ways of looking. Some of our vulnerability to feeling badly because of our appearance is related to the fact that our sense of self is not reinforced by networks of relations in communities by what we do, and how we treat others, as much as it is by how strangers and casual acquaintances perceive us.

There is much feminist literature on the dangers of an addiction to beauty for women, and there is an increasing awareness of the ever more pervasive ways that that men, and nonbinary people, are also swept up into the capitalist machine that generates so much misery about looks. With some forms of social media, it is increasingly difficult to avoid the everyday beauty pageant of life. Increased use of social media is associated with increasing levels in the population of serious body dysmorphia from viewing the filtered and cleaned up images of our friends and associates.

There are many things we can do as individuals to resist the pull toward self-hatred that the culture pushes us toward. The simple act of not looking at magazines or television with ads in them used to be a high impact practice for increasing oneself sense of well-being. Now, we also need to stay off social media. But the first step in finding joy in our bodies is being aware of the problem. It helps to be part of a subculture that recognizes the variety of human beauties, and the beauty of ways of being in one's body, clothing, hair and face, nails, that doesn't require high levels of wasteful consumption, but that still allows us to feel attractive, to be recognized as beautiful by others. We need to live much of our lives in parallel subcultures and communities where beauty images are less toxic.

The Aesthetics of a Sustainable World

Spreading an aesthetic of a life full of joy and meaning and a sense of sufficiency was core to the work of nineteenth-century British artist and philosopher, William Morris. Morris promoted a political vision of a society that would support satisfying and well-lived lives for all. He saw industrial labor as alienated labor that made people's lives miserable. He harkened back to craft labor, and the beauty and joy in making things and of enjoying life that were part of preindustrial British society.

As an artist, he developed designs for furniture, wallpaper, and household objects that were affordable, made with pleasurable craft processes, durable, and a pleasure to live with. He designed beautiful fabrics and wallpaper patterns that were warm and inviting and reminded one of the beauties of natural life forms. His work helped heal a separation from nature that people living in industrial towns experienced. He helped people find beauty in everyday things and pleasure in living.

Morris saw capitalism as destroying beauty in life and destroying the ability of working-class people to experience joy. He wrote that

> Nothing made by man's [sic] hand can be indifferent: it must either be beautiful and elevating, or ugly and degrading; and those things that are without art are so aggressively; they wound it by their existence.[6]

For Morris there is no individual solution to the ugliness that capitalism brings. Capitalism degrades the life of working people. It robs them of the pleasures of everyday existence it makes all the things they interact with ugly.

For the wealthy, it makes their art irrelevant to life and leads to lives devoid of meaning.

William Morris worried that the imperatives in capitalism to produce ever more cheaply would lead to a decimation of joy in labor and in our relationships to the physical objects that are parts of our lives. In one of his most quotable phrases, he asked, "Was it all to end in a counting-house on top of a cinder-heap"?[7] Morris has a lot to teach us about an aesthetics of sufficiency. It is not an aesthetics of sacrifice nor is it a status-driven aesthetics. It is an aesthetics of an integrated world of work and leisure for pleasure and joy, where everyone is invited to enjoy the objects we live with, from their production to their use in our lives. He calls for an aesthetics of well-being based on sufficiency.

Morris' aesthetics is based on pleasure, but it is not a hedonistic, addictive, consumption-driven pleasure. It is a pleasure in seeing the connections between things; in the production and consumption of goods, and the sociality associated with those goods. It is a pleasure in the human and environmental connections between ourselves and the rest of our world. Many people try to create those sorts of noncommercial bonds in community fairs and festivals, by making and listening to music, by noticing the world around us and insisting it be beautiful and full of joy. The solution for Morris was to end alienated labor, to have work involve pleasure and pride in making beautiful well-designed and useful things, and to have the time to appreciate those things.

We can see something of a sustainable aesthetics in food cultures where they haven't been destroyed by capitalism. In 1999, I visited a women's weaving cooperative in the region of Chiapas Mexico that was run by the Zapatista movement. There, people were working in community making traditional crafts as a cooperative and selling some of them to the world market. While we were there, we were served a meal of tacos made of peas and other locally grown vegetables. The meal was delicious and none of the food in it involved exploited labor or the exploitation of nature. As we were leaving the cooperative, military helicopters flew overhead and some of us were taken in to the police station for questioning. The utopian moment I experienced having lunch at the cooperative was hemmed in by the forces working to destroy those cooperatives in the interest of protecting a very different world.

That meal in Chiapas was different in so many ways from one eaten in our everyday lives in industrial societies, where we know that many of the ingredients in our meals come via farmworkers who grew and picked the food and were underpaid and exposed to pesticides, where we know that if it includes meat that the animals were raised in torturous conditions and that the workers who slaughtered the animals were working in dangerous and inhumane conditions. When we eat a conventional modern meal, if we are to enjoy it, we need to close our eyes to the fabric of connections that flow between ourselves and the forces that brought that meal to our mouth.

An aesthetics of a sustainable world would encourages us to think through and meditate on the long chain of connections between the food one is eating, the pleasure of the taste, and the dense network of relationships that go into that act of eating, and a reflection on the ways that those connections include pain and harm. Eventually we might be able to live with our eyes wide open to the relations and connections around us and feel joy in the health of those connections. As we are able to develop forms of living that connect in healthy ways to the material substrate of our existence, we are able to feel deeply into the interrelations that constitute our world. Opening our eyes to the fabric of connections between ourselves and the social processes through which we live is part of building a world of enough.

Shifting Wasteful Consumption

In San Mateo County, California, where I live, advocates worked hard to create a new public electricity supplier that provides everyone electricity from renewable sources at no extra cost. I turn off the light when I leave a room and have low wattage light bulbs, but those individual lifestyle actions do not have anywhere near the impact of the work people did together to bring us a new electricity supplier.

In the past 20 years, recognizing the power of collective action, and concerned with the race and class biases in the environmental movement, environmental advocates have shifted their focus from the individual lifestyle choices of people with money and a lot of choices, to the social systems and structures that drive environmental devastation and that provide fewer and worse choices for low-income people and people of color. Environmentalists are now asking deeper questions about how to shift those contexts to make personal choices more productive. Rather than asking people to spend more on light bulbs, they are focusing more on how to deliver cheap renewable energy to everyone. Rather than looking at each of us as an individual consumer, they are starting to look at the contexts that feed us the options we chose between.

Our consumption choices take place within a complex matrix of relationships. If we want to shift how people consume, we need to attend to the things that make less wasteful choices more appealing and easier. Researchers working in this area are beginning to shift the focus from the individual consumer to the "practices" that need to shift. According to Dale Evans, Andrew McMeekin, and David Southerton:

> many existing approaches to sustainable consumption frame the problem as a matter of sovereign consumer behavior and present the solution as

one of influencing choices and persuading individuals to behave in ways that are less environmentally damaging.

In contrast, they argue that people make choices within the context of shared social practices, and so it is important to look at the way individual consumer choices are wrapped up in networks of action that involve "the dynamics of everyday life; social relations; material culture; socio-technical systems; cultural conventions; and shared understandings."[8]

In their article they share the example of "Cool Biz," a very successful program in Japan to reduce the use of air conditioning in government offices. The government could have done a campaign to tell everyone to turn down the AC. Or they could have created a rule that it must be turned down and made people miserable and resentful of environmental regulations. But policy makers realized that part of what was driving the need for extreme cooling was the standard dress code for men to wear full business suits, even in summer.

And so, the government did integrated work to shift the whole matrix of the practice that was driving wasteful air conditioning use. A new dress code was instituted in which ties and blazers were replaced with lightweight summer clothing made from "breathable" fibers. In order to promote and normalize this dress code, the ministry worked with designers and retailers to develop appropriate attire as well as organizing fashion shows in which high profile ministers and attractive young people modeled the garments.

The authors explain the implications of this for policy makers: if you want to shift a practice, you need to investigate the ways that aspects of social actions are interconnected and not focus on individuals as your main unit of analysis. Those wanting to shift a social practice need to focus on "the importance of targeting the multiple activities and components which together configure practices as entities."

The strands of individual and collective action are woven together in many complicated ways. Years ago, my students were involved in a campaign to bring bus rapid transit (BRT) to the highly suburban area where our college, De Anza, is located. The organizers we were working with were very clear that people would stop driving only if the bus could be faster than a car and only if people could come to see riding the bus as a positive option. Part of the campaign was to improve the BRT busses' image: they had Wi-Fi and comfortable seats and looked nice. Part of the advocates' job was to change the rules so that the busses would be faster. The other part was to make riding the bus seem cool.

As my students at De Anza were advocating, first for bus passes, and then later for BRT, many of them rode the terrible bus system we had. For some who couldn't afford a car, it was their only option. But a few others rode the bus as a matter of principle. I always thought that for those few students, the work they did to transform the system was more important than their individual choice to ride our underfunded bus system and that their actual riding was unnecessary. And yet, I have come to see that there was something important about their living the reality of a slow bus system every day. The more obvious effect was to give them credibility in the fight for a better system. But the other part, which I had not really taken seriously enough, was that by riding the bus they were seeing every day the barriers that needed to be overcome to improve the system. They were living the practice that needed shifting and seeing all of the ways that the practice needed to change. There is a kind of knowledge that comes only from close experience with the ways that systems fail, and activists with that detailed knowledge are in a good position to advocate for ways to change those systems.

Living the reality of a change you want others to make can be complicated. I recently decided to not fly unnecessarily. When I mention that I am not flying, I hope it encourages some of the people I speak with to ask themselves if they should fly as much as they do. But I also know that I need to be careful, because it is also quite possible that my personal choice might trigger feelings of guilt or resentment and might actually encourage others to fly more, just to spite self-righteous people like me.

I have been a vegetarian since I was 14. For almost my whole life, it has been common that when tell someone that I didn't care to eat something because I was a vegetarian, they would start to tell me about their meat-eating habits. And those stories often seem to come with a lot of guilt and discomfort. I always try to walk them out of their guilt and describe my choice to not eat meat in the most benign way possible, because I don't want to be socially rejected as a self-righteous person who tries to make other people feel bad. And yet I believe that making the choices we think are right, and talking about them in matter-of-fact ways, without being aggressive or preachy, is important. Thoughtful messaging can avoid backlash and can lead to shifts in cultural norms.

Even more significant, though, is when we move outward from our individual consumer choices, and talking about those choices, to the ways that our individual choices are enabled, and sometimes hindered, by the fabric of practices that connect us to other people, and when we work to transform that fabric. Part of the whole practice of going on vacation for middle-class people is wrapped up with wasteful forms of consumerism and driven by capitalist forms of desire and marketing. Middle-class people fly to faraway places, post about it on social media, and come home and share stories of how much fun it was. COVID-19 pushed many people to explore more intensively the places near where they live. Many people who fly for vacation are nowhere near exhausting the possibilities in places nearby. What are the social forces that drive middle-class people to take vacations in faraway places? What do we need to do to develop a social imagination that builds and reinforces the fun of a "staycation" or a vacation by train?

Many middle-class people also fly too much as part of their work lives. I am a member of an academic organization that has traditionally had a national conference somewhere in the US every two years. The organization had a virtual conference in 2021 because of COVID-19. There were a few good things that come from in-person conferences that I missed at the 2021 conference. There was none of the fun of going out eating and drinking with new friends and old friends who I only see at those conferences. There was none of the chance for conversations with people in the hallways or after a session. But I was also struck by the unexpected positives that came from the conference being virtual. I was able to invite comment on my work from a colleague from Mexico who never would have traveled to that particular conference if it had been in person in the US. There was also a whole crew of students who presented, who probably would not have had the funding to attend in person. The conference became more accessible.

There is a movement developing to encourage people who organize conferences to make them more virtual. The journal *Nature* published the article "An Analysis of Ways to Decarbonize Conference Travel after COVID-19,"[9] which outlined the importance of shifting to virtual conferences and the many of the benefits of doing so. It turns out that conferences are a significant source of global emissions. Someone sent me that article and I shared it with the organizers of my biennial conference and made the case for why the conference should be at least partially virtual, even if we are done with COVID-19 restrictions by then. My personal decision to not fly much helped focus me on the network of relationships I am embedded in. I don't plan to fly, and I don't want to miss the next conference.

Goal Blue is an organization in China that focuses on shifting the cultural meaning of meat consumption and car driving. In much of the global south both of those things are high status forms of consumption, and as people get enough money, they generally shift to eating more meat and to owning a car. But, of course, if everyone buys a car then everyone is stuck in traffic, and life is pretty miserable. And if everyone who is middle-class in the world eats as much meat as the average US citizen, it will be impossible to cut emissions to half by 2030 and to zero by 2050.

Goal Blue's slogan is "Good for me. Good for earth" and they use advertising techniques to make less wasteful practices look glamorous, ethical, and fun. Since launching in 2016, Goal Blue has produced prominent public advertising campaigns featuring some of China's most famous film and TV stars, gained tens of millions of video views with top trending topics on WeChat, brought nutrition and gardening education pilots into hundreds of schools, and partnered with numerous sports and entertainment companies to produce large-scale public events.

Like many organizations working to shift social meanings around consumption, Goal Blue does not focus on "being a vegetarian" or signing a pledge to never fly or never drive. Instead, the focus is on the benefits of engaging in other practices that are better for the earth. They want you to do more of the good things and less of the bad ones. Turning less carbon-intensive choices into an identity "being a vegetarian" or "a person who does not fly" sets the bar too high and can create barriers to the spread of better practices. In the US, many people are advocating for Meat-Free Mondays, the beauty of staycations, the value of taking public transit, biking, or walking once a week, rather than complete renunciation of carbon-intensive consumerism.

As we engage in healthier practices and push to make those practices more convenient, we need to also work to shift the meaning of things, such that for example it is not a sign of success to drive a car, eat meat, or travel by plane on vacation. We need to also change the context that makes those better choices more convenient, more attractive, cheaper, and more socially acceptable. None of us exists as an autonomous individual. Instead, we are all members of social networks which we create, enact, and reproduce everyday by our actions. Reweaving the webs of our relations such that we can all live well together is crucial for our survival. A small part of that reweaving should be to cut down on being wasteful consumers in places where we can.

When Individual Change Becomes Cultural Change

Each of us is a member of society and how we act influences the whole in a few different ways. One is additive. If my carbon emission goes down, then world emissions go down by that much. And yet that basic additive impact is pretty small on a world of 8 billion people. A bigger impact can come from the ways my actions as an individual can send signals to others and get them to question what they do and can cause ripples in the culture and, by changing social expectations it can change the attitudes of many more people. Because status and status anxiety are such big drivers of a world without enough, shifting the drivers of status must to be core of our strategies to get to a world of enough.

In addition to acting in ways that model change and inspire others, we can work intentionally to shift social meanings. We can also produce art, give our opinions in blogs and podcasts, and spread media that resonates with the messages we like. We can be cultural activists. Many of us do a bit of cultural activism on our social media, through what we decide to share and the content we create and share. We can work together to promote the idea of enough and the beauty in a life lived in commitment to providing enough for everyone, while living within the ecological limits for the planet. We can work to develop and propagate narratives of what we expect from ourselves and others to be considered ethical in the current world of multiple and intersecting crises we are immersed in.

Another thing that gets in the way of low consumption lifestyles is the widespread belief that if we don't keep consuming, other people won't have jobs and so won't be able to live well. As we will see in Chapter 4, there are ways that we think about the economy that keep us from seeing a pathway to a world of enough for everyone. It turns out that we don't need to keep consuming more for people to have access to what they need. In fact, the reality is quite the opposite.

A few lessons from this:

1 We cannot shop our way to a sustainable world.
2 We always live in community with others and our individual choices about how we live our life does have an impact on those around us.
3 For people who have enough, it is possible to feel a sense of abundance, if one detaches to some extent, from mainstream culture.
4 For those who already have enough, choosing to consume less is easier for people who do not carry the trauma of disdain from mainstream culture based on class, race, and gender.
5 Policy changes such as a high minimum wage, and strong public goods, make it much easier to live well without being trapped in our jobs.
6 There are practices we can engage in, such as turning away from social media and advertising, that make it easier to live joyfully and accept the bodies we have.
7 If we want an anti-consumerist lifestyle to spread, it needs to look attractive and appealing.
8 Lifestyle choices take place in networks of interrelated practices, and there is much that we can do to shift those networks of practices.
9 We can each make choices, for our own happiness, to detach from the toxic world of consumer culture and status striving.

Notes

1 These statements are made up and are intended to represent the kinds of things people say on the subject of enough.
2 Adel Daoud. 2018. "Unifying studies of scarcity, abundance, and sufficiency." *Ecological Economics*, 147, 208–217.
3 Adel Daoud. 2011. "The modus vivendi of material simplicity: Counteracting scarcity via the deflation of wants." *Review of Social Economy*, 69.3, 275–305, 275.
4 Adrienne Maree Brown. 2019. *Pleasure Activism*. AK Press, page 10.
5 Robert H. Frank. 2001. *Luxury Fever: Why Money Fails to Satisfy in an Era of Excess*. Simon and Schuster, page 168, 203.
6 William Morris. 2004. "Hopes and Fears for Art. Lectures on Art and Industry." *The Collected Works of William Morris: Volume 22*. Adamant Media Corporation, page 56.

7 William Morris. 2020. *How I Became a Socialist*. Ed. Owen Holland. Verso, page 171.

8 Dale Evans, Andrew McMeekin, and David Southerton. 2011. "Sustainable consumption, behaviour change policies, and theories of practice," *International Review of Behaviour Change Initiatives*. The Scottish Government, page 114.

9 Nature. 2020. "An Analysis of Ways to Decarbonize Conference Travel after COVID-19," July 15.

Chapter 4

Economics Based on Scarcity and Infinite Growth

Scarcity: The resources that we value—time, money, labor, tools, land, and raw materials—exist in limited supply. There are simply never enough resources to meet all our needs and desires. This condition is known as scarcity.

Economics: The study of how humans make choices under conditions of scarcity.[1]

A drink priced at $10,000 comes with a pre-selected diamond sparkling on the bottom. What's the point? Hotel officials say it's a perfect way to propose marriage or mark any other special occasion. Nothing says love like a big rock under the olive, right?[2]

If we want to get to a world of enough, we need economic tools to help us understand the nature of our shared world, help us find pathways to ensuring that there is no poverty, help us find ways to ensure that we leave enough for the natural world, and help us find ways to ensure that people have the ability to live good lives. The word *economics* comes from the Greek root *oikos*, which means home. For Aristotle, economics was the study of how we manage our home. This is a beautiful way to think of what economics could be: the study of the best ways to manage the resources we use to take care of our lives. As we will see in Chapter 5, many economists take that approach and are working to develop the tools we need to get to a world of enough.

In contrast to that approach, contemporary mainstream economics generally defines the discipline more narrowly as the study of how to allocate scarce resources. And it starts from a few key assumptions that doom it to not being helpful for getting us to a world of enough. It starts from an assumption of scarcity, from the assumption that human beings are fundamentally self-interested and avaricious, and from the assumption that what is good for generating profit is what is good for our economies. Mainstream economics puts a lock on our imagination and leads to policy prescriptions that drive us way

DOI: 10.4324/9781003354871-5

from a world of enough. What is taught in economics classrooms matters, because those ideas become part of the general set of assumptions accepted widely in society, and they are core ideas for those making social policy and telling us what is possible and what is not.

After the global economic crash of 2008, which mainstream economists did not predict, graduate students at the University of Manchester, in the United Kingdom, kicked off the International Student Initiative for Pluralism in Economics. That organization published an open letter in 2014, which began:

> It is not only the world economy that is in crisis. The teaching of economics is in crisis too, and this crisis has consequences far beyond the university walls. What is taught shapes the minds of the next generation of policymakers, and therefore shapes the societies we live in. We, over 65 associations of economics students from over 30 different countries, believe it is time to reconsider the way economics is taught. We are dissatisfied with the dramatic narrowing of the curriculum that has taken place over the last couple of decades. This lack of intellectual diversity does not only restrain education and research. It limits our ability to contend with the multidimensional challenges of the 21st century—from financial stability, to food security and climate change. The real world should be brought back into the classroom, as well as debate and a pluralism of theories and methods. Such change will help renew the discipline and ultimately create a space in which solutions to society's problems can be generated.[3]

Part of the drive toward narrowness in the dominant approach is a desire for economics to function like the natural sciences. Many economists are attracted to the idea that they are using clear mathematical models to objectively study a well-defined aspect of reality that is ruled by fixed laws. To put themselves into this position, they create a simple rule-bound thing in their models called "the economy." They then work their models to help figure out what is best for that thing. Philosophers call this practice of turning something complex, and determined by social processes, into something fixed and stable "reification." As a result of this reification, economics becomes the study of what is good for that thing, instead of being a messy and value laden investigation into the best ways to manage our home, so that we can live well together. The mainstream of the discipline claims that questions of how we should live, and what is good for the environment, or for society, are outside its purview.

The mainstream economic model starts with a few fundamental assumptions and then builds extremely complex mathematical models based on those assumptions. There is a little empirical study of whether or not those theoretical models are able to predict real-world events or help us solve our real-world problems. In recent years some of the world's most prominent economists have won Nobel prizes for challenging those assumptions.[4] And yet, most mainstream economics textbooks carry on as if that research never happened.

Policy makers continue to use its imperatives to make political arguments for how we should manage society, while saying they are merely following science. And when regular people ask questions about how the world can be, their sense of what is possible is constrained by these unhelpful frameworks. This chapter explores some of the most dangerous assumptions behind the dominant approach to economics.

The Rational Maximizer Who Can Never Get Enough

Mainstream economics is based on the philosophy of utilitarianism. One of utilitarianism's most important founders, Jeremy Bentham, claimed that the best society was one which gave the greatest good to the greatest number. For him, people can be understood to be always making choices to maximize their utility. Bentham went on to elaborate in detail the "utils" one would gain by engaging in different activities. Human beings are seen in mainstream economic theory as "utility maximisers." We can know what is in a person's interest by watching how they spend their money. We can assume that they are constantly maximizing their utility in the choices they make. Their getting more of that they want means they are better off. Bentham argued that we should not make judgments about what a person wants.

Inherent in this utilitarian foundation for economics is a deeply value laden and deeply flawed notion of human well-being, desire, and motivation. The view of happiness embedded in mainstream economics tends toward hedonism. Happiness is about getting what a person wants. The idea that what is good for a person is what that person spends their money on has the virtue of being easily quantifiable. And it has the virtue of being able to be analyzed without anyone telling anyone else how they should live. And yet, by focusing on market behavior as the most important thing about human life choices, it renders invisible the social bonds and processes that present us with market choices, the political processes that shape markets, the actions of others that stimulate our desires, and the reality that different ones of us have different amounts of money to spend.

If a Black woman in the US can't buy a house because a racist banking system won't give her a loan, the logic of economics only looks at that complex situation when she "chooses" to rent instead of buying. And when it is not profitable for anyone to build rental housing, and so she must pay half her income for an apartment, economic logic only sees her "choosing" to live in a crummy apartment a long distance from her job. If a white man thinks his yacht needs to be bigger than his friend's yacht, then he is maximizing his utility by buying that bigger yacht. Mainstream economics says that society should be run in ways that allow him to increase his utility, because we should not make value judgments about how people live.

Claiming to be an objective science, economics looks at what increases utility. Questioning this logic is seen by the discipline of economics as oppressive social meddling. And yet, putting the utility maximization of individuals as a goal, rather than, for example poverty reduction, is clearly a value judgment. Mainstream economics assumes that people are separate, not connected to others, that they are purely motivated by what is good for themselves, and that they are unconcerned with what is good for others. And yet there is no evidence that people work this way, and a lot of evidence that they don't.

Building an economic model for how we should run society on the basis of that set of assumptions becomes a self-fulfilling prophecy. If you build your model for how to organize our common relations on the basis competition between individuals, you will end up with social forms that don't take our common interests seriously. That way of framing our economic situation helps drive the idea that scarcity is inevitable. The rational maximizer is always hungry for more. By not asking questions about how we should create and distribute the things we need to have good lives for all of us, the mainstream of economics rules out of bounds the difficult and important questions that need to be addressed by economic policy.

One of the most pernicious concepts that has grown out of this nexus of ideas is the concept of pareto optimality. Italian economist Wilfredo Pareto, who was a fascist sympathizer, argued that, because we are not allowed to make any judgments about the good life for humans, and because the goal of economics is to increase utility, when deciding between two different social policies, the one that increases utility without decreasing the utility of any individual is the best one. So, for example, a tax policy which took wealth from the top .01% and used it to build housing for the poor is not a good policy, because by taking from the wealthy, it is not pareto optimal. Pareto optimality imposes arbitrary limits on social policy. With no argument for why it is a good idea, it simply asserts that we should only approve social policies which can find a way to improve the well-being of the poor without taking from the wealthy. This is obviously a value statement, and there is no scientific basis for arguing that pareto optimality is good for society. It is a deeply reactionary value statement, offered to students of economics as a scientific principle.

Scarcity

Mainstream economics starts from the assumptions that there isn't enough in the world to go around. It defines the job of economics as finding ways to allocate scarce goods, it also adds the proviso that, as an objective science, it should not make judgments about what people should want.

From this it concludes that markets are the best ways to allocate resources. As the economics textbook quoted above states, "There are simply never enough resources to meet all our needs and desires ... Economics is the study of how humans make choices under conditions of scarcity."[5] Or as another widely used textbooks put it, without scarcity "all goods would be free, like sand in the desert or seawater at the beach. All prices would be zero, and markets would be unnecessary. Indeed, economics would no longer be a useful subject."[6]

In the ideal model of a market society, no one needs to make any value judgments about anyone else's purchases. If people are buying certain things, then businesses will produce more of those things, and as the markets magically match supply with demand, society will produce the things needed to maximize people's utility. More of certain kinds of food will be produced if that is what people want, and if they express that want by paying for it. In this way, mainstream economists argue, food will be distributed in ways that maximize the utility of all participants. Markets are said to balance supply and demand, by allocating resources based on how much people want something.

In 2015, rents in Pacifica, California, where I live, were going up so fast that people were being displaced from our town and our whole region. Some of us worked to put a ballot measure to the town to put a cap on rent increases. As we were campaigning for the initiative, one of the most common arguments against us was that we didn't understand the most basic truth in economics. Everyone who takes Economics 101 knows that you can't set prices "artificially." Instead, you need to let the markets work out a balance between supply and demand. And the natural price will be the price that works the best. We were called fools for not understanding that very basic truth.

This simple idea, that left undisturbed, markets will find an optimal balance between supply and demand, and therefore that public policies should not impact prices is a core principle in mainstream economics. George Akerlof won the Nobel Prize in Economics in 2001 for proving that markets don't work that way in real life. The article that won him the prize, which was rejected several times before finding a publisher, showed that buyers and sellers generally don't have the same information, and so prices can easily be manipulated.[7] There are a wide variety of forces that impact the prices of goods. There is the information that people have, there is advertising, there is monopoly power, there are government subsidies and regulations that always and inevitably shape markets. Increasingly there is the power of finance capital that has a huge impact on how and where money flows. It is not the case that in a capitalist society, resources are allocated based on the laws of supply and demand.

In the rental market, at the present time, there is so much finance capital looking for a safe place to rest, that the world is full of vacant housing units whose investor owners cannot be bothered to rent them out. Rent control, and the emerging tool of taxing vacant units, are policies designed to protect access to housing for those whose interests are not served by unregulated markets. The preferred solution to the housing crisis among followers of mainstream economics is to loosen regulations to encourage the building of more market rate houses. And yet, at the present time, that is not likely to lower the costs of housing at the lower end of the market. It just creates more places for finance capital to be parked.

The most significant way that the laws of supply and demand don't work to get resources allocated in the best way possible is that markets don't respond to the demand of those without money. If I want a martini with a diamond in it and I have enough money, the market will supply that. But if I am on the brink of starvation and have no money, the market does not care about the pain in my body. It only responds to "effective demand" which is demand backed by money. The speculator who is able to hoard huge quantities of food is maximizing his utility by doing so, his desire for food can be infinite, and markets will continue to give him what increases his utility. That rational maximizer always wants more utils, and more is always better.

The theory of declining marginal utility says that generally once a person gets enough, their utility for the next martini with a diamond in it will be less than the utility they got from the first one, and so at a certain point it isn't worth it to the consumer to buy another one. But in a society with high levels of inequality, where status comes from having more, and where profit comes from finding new things for people to want, the laws of supply and demand will not allocate resources in ways that are socially beneficial. For the so-called "law" of supply and demand to work effectively to get people the things they need, their demand needs to be backed by money. People's desires for more need not be infinite. Buyers and sellers need to have perfect information. Suppliers need to have a self-interest in producing the things people need.

In 2020, there were 580,466 homeless people in the US and 15 million vacant housing units.[8] In 2019 the group Moms for Housing made headlines when three mothers and their children, all of whom had been homeless in Oakland California, moved into an empty house on Magnolia Street. In prior years, Oakland had been devastated by the foreclosure crisis that began in 2008. As many homes were foreclosed on, and families were displaced, investment firms swooped in and bought large numbers of homes, sometimes 50 at a time at auctions.[9] The house the moms moved into had been empty for two years when they moved in. Moms for Housing succeeded in putting the issues of vacancy and financial speculation on the map as an aspect of the crisis in homelessness.

There are many people who believe that the most important solution to homelessness is to promote the building of more market rate housing to get supply to meet demand. They point out that many vacant units are in disrepair, many are people's second homes, and there are all sorts of complex reasons why people end up living on the streets, and getting them into safe housing is a complex issue. While all of that is true, it is also true that: there are enough homes for everyone to have one; the housing market is not working to provide homes for everyone; and policies other than building more market rate housing will be needed to get everyone access to the shelter they deserve as a human right.

Just as homelessness is a political problem having to do with the ways that resources are distributed, something similar can be said about hunger. For every year in recorded history, the world has produced enough food for everyone on the planet to have a healthy diet. Even in the worst famines, the problem was political. The people who needed food didn't have the power to get the food they needed. Amartya Sen has argued that at no time in history has there been a famine in a country with a democratic political system.[10] Famines are caused by people who control food resources not sharing them and those needing food not having the political leverage to make the system meet their needs.

When the potato crop was destroyed by a blight in Ireland in 1845–1852 people starved to death and emigrated because of hunger. At that time, the granaries in Ireland were full of rye, but the British landowners who owned that grain withheld it. By starving the Irish, they were able to take even more land from the Irish than they had already taken.[11] In *Late Victorian Holocausts: El Niño Famines and the Making of the Third World*, speaking of a famine in the Berar region of India, Mike Davis writes that "During the famine of 1899–1900, when 143,000 Beraris died directly from starvation, the province exported not only thousands of bales of cotton but an incredible 747,000 bushels of grain."[12] In both of these cases, markets were not able to feed people because the people had no money to buy the food, and those who didn't want them to get the food, chose to let them starve. There was no scarcity of food. Markets did not work to prevent starvation.

By restricting its scope to helping markets distribute scarce goods, the mainstream economic paradigm keeps a few very important questions away from its purview. It doesn't look at the ways that a profit-based economic system encourages people's desires to be insatiable. It doesn't take seriously the notion from the Universal Declaration of Human Rights that there are basic minimum needs for food, clothing, and shelter, which should be attended to as rights. Mainstream economics allows the desire for a third house to be equivalent to the need for shelter. And as ecological economists, such as Herman Daly argue, this approach doesn't take seriously the physical limits of the natural world, which the economy is embedded in, and so it doesn't allow economists to ask questions about how to stay within the ecological limits of the planet.[13]

Mainstream economics says that markets need to decide how to distribute food and homes. The rational maximizer should be allowed to follow his whims. How much he desires a home, and the free market that sets prices should be, should be what decides who gets to live where and eat what. But as we have seen, that rational maximizer always wants more. Allowing his desires to set policy creates the situation of perpetual scarcity that mainstream economists say should be the main focus of their work.

Adel Daoud has done work to help economists get past the simplistic approach to scarcity built into mainstream economics. He argues that economists should look at scarcity, abundance, and sufficiency (SAS) as an interrelated set of dynamics, and they should work to understand their relationships. He proposes a unified approach to analyzing problems of how resources are allocated. Rather than just focusing on the ways that markets allocate scarce goods, economists should also look at what makes a good become scarce in people's minds, how to ensure a sufficiency of the things people need, and what the things are that make people feel that they have enough. As we saw in Chapter 3, Daoud has studied people who work to decrease their desires for more and so are able to find ways to live in a state of abundance, within cultures where others experience an unceasing desire for more and so live with a sense of scarcity.[14]

Daoud's approach asks economists to look at any problem of how to deal with resources from within a holistic framework and to ask deeper questions than the discipline of economics typically asks. How can we make the things we want be abundant? What allows us to feel a sense of sufficiency in some things? What are the best ways to allocate those things which are unavoidably scarce? The discipline of economics needs to set itself the ambitious goal of helping us understand how to achieve a world that works for everyone. It needs to stop throwing up its hands at these questions by claiming that it has no theory of the good life and that it only analyzes what is "best for the economy."

If we begin from the presumption that there is not enough and that markets are the best ways to decide who gets what, then there will never be enough to go around. As we have seen, many forms of scarcity are an artifact of our approach to economics. This approach gives up on what should be the most important work of economics. It bakes into our social policies ways of making those hard decisions that favor the wealthy. If people are understood as rational maximizers who always want more, then we will always have scarcity. And, worse, that set of assumptions encourages us to take the needs of a billionaire to have another yacht as seriously as we take the needs of someone without a place to live to have shelter.

The Feminist Critique of the Definition of "the Economy"

Feminist economics has been producing important work that deeply questions the foundations of economic theory for almost 50 years. Many of its insights are important for an economics of enough. The most crucial insight

62 Economics Based on Scarcity and Infinite Growth

from feminist economics is that the economy is not just the money economy. New Zealand economist and legislator Marilyn Waring wrote the most influential early popular book on the subject, *If Women Counted: A New Feminist Economics.* In it, she showed that a huge part of what we do to meet our needs in human society has nothing to do with capitalist markets.

People clean for others, they cook for them, they make things and share them, they care for children, elders, and the sick. If I take care of my neighbor's children and they cook for me, my neighbor and I are not seen by mainstream economics as engaging in productive activity. But if I worked in daycare center and was paid, and then used that money to eat in a restaurant, my work, and my spending, would both count as economic activity and would be calculated as part of Gross Domestic Product (GDP). The work traditionally done by women is invisible to mainstream economics, and yet it is some of the most important, and in many cases the most satisfying, and ecologically sustainable, work we do to meet our human needs.

Much of that work can be called caregiving labor. Nancy Folbre has done important work finding ways to quantify and value that form of labor. And yet the kinds of activities that people engage in that should be recognized, valued, and promoted, go beyond just the provision of care. Mary Robinson has argued that "nearly 70 percent of the food consumed around the world is produced by millions of smallholder and subsistence farmers across Asia and Africa—the vast majority women."[15] Much of that food production, if it is done for the use of the family, is not counted by mainstream economics.

Folbre has developed a categorization of the kinds of work that exist and shows how caregiving labor is wrapped up in them. Her list includes: wage work, self-employment work, unpaid work, nonmarket work, and paid and unpaid care work.[16] Because the notion of caregiving labor cuts across all of these categories of work, it doesn't make sense to use the term caregiving labor to describe all of the aspects of work that are neither done for a capitalist market nor controlled by a state. A catch-all term for those other aspects of work is *provisioning*.

The provisioning aspects of our economies are huge. In one wonderful example, Folbre cites a study which shows that if the breastmilk babies are fed in Australia were replaced by commercial alternatives, it would count for 1% of GDP.[17] The things people do to meet their needs outside the market and the state such as, caring for elders, canning vegetables one grew oneself, farming for one's family, or breastfeeding babies, are huge contributors to human well-being. Unfortunately, when policy-makers try to promote "development," they often suppose that means shifting more production into market-based parts of the economy, which they see as advances because it can be captured by measures such as GDP. Much of development policy is based on a misperception of the value of provisioning that grows from how we measure our economies.

Economics Based on Scarcity and Infinite Growth   63

In *A Postcapitalist Politics,* J.K. Gibson-Graham argues that even in highly industrialized societies, more than half of the things we do to meet our needs are done outside the realm of wage labor.[18] In less industrialized economies the proportion is even higher. By measuring our economies on the basis of GDP we are valuing and encouraging activity that takes place in the sphere of capitalist throughput and making invisible the crucial web of relationships that we rely on. Feminist economists argue for developing tools to measure the success of economic policies by focusing on human well-being and taking the nonpaid aspects of the economy seriously.

Often societies which support noncommercial ways of taking care of our needs are much more rewarding to live in than ones where everyone needs to buy and sell, and work in wage labor, to meet those needs. Waring argues that we need to find ways to acknowledge, value, and support the work done in the nonmonetary parts of our economy. Feminist economists have worked to bring household labor, barter, and sharing into the conversation when we talk about economics. These provisioning aspects of our economies are invisible to mainstream economists because they do not involve buying and selling. They are invisible to socialist economists because they do not involve the government, or what social scientists call "the state." Whether or not they are seen as part of the economy depends on how one defines "the economy."

Our contemporary idea of an "economy" is based on the ways that capitalism turns "the market" into a part of life that is measured and separated from the rest of the fabric of life. There is nothing wrong with markets making some social decision about how to allocate resources, as long as we don't fall into a "market fundamentalism" that supposes market should be "free" to run society in the interests of profits.[19] But we end up with deep confusion about how society works if we suppose that "the economy" is by definition market activity. One mistake that many socialists make is that they accept the definition of what is an economy that grows out of the experience of capitalism and then argue that "the economy" should be run by the state instead of markets. This view perpetuates the invisibility of household labor and other forms of provisioning. Feminist economists have argued that the very idea of "the economy" as a clearly definable part of social life is an artifact of a capitalist economy.

Human beings do all sorts of things to live their lives, meet their needs, and make themselves happy. Precapitalist human societies did not have a separate part of society called an economy. Rather, making and sharing food, and building shelter were all wrapped up in the whole fabric of social relationships. Feminist such as Gibson-Graham and Waring argue that we should have an expansive definition of what an economy is which encompasses non-market and non-state activities. On this view economic activity is activity directed to meeting our needs. But that definition also becomes slippery, because once we think of all of the ways that human beings meet their needs, in some ways all aspects of society are wrapped up in that.[20] In a capitalist market-based society, therapists are paid to have caring and supportive conversations with others. Does the conversation I have with a friend count as caring labor? Ann Ferguson argues that it should, and that the concept of labor should be expanded to include nurturing labor and even sexual "labor." For her, labor is defined as the things we do to meet our needs. She is interested in the forms of exploitation and unequal exchange that surround the things we do to meet our needs, in capitalist wage labor, as well as in caring labor. [21]

Most thinkers working to stretch the idea of an economy beyond the bounds of the capitalist market allow some flexibility in how they define economic activity. Thinkers working in this area shift their focus to understand the things we need to do such that our needs are met well. They ask what leads to good outcomes for society, using wholistic well-being indicators, and work backwards from that to ask what the social policies are that lead to improvements in those indicators. In this way economics becomes not about just market activity, the state sector, or even caregiving labor. Instead, it becomes the study of how we manage society's resources to ensure that our needs are met.

Measuring the Health of an Economy

GDP measures the monetary value of things bought and sold within a given geographic area, such as a country. As we saw in Chapter 2, GDP was originally intended as one part of a Keynesian analysis to help predict and manage boom and bust cycles. But over time, it has come to be the most widely used measure of the overall health of an economy. When GDP growth is the goal of economics, policies are favored that lead to more work and more consumption, and that often goes along with more environmental destruction, and the promotion of more insatiable desires. GDP does not ask us to look at issues of how wealth and income are distributed. It does not promote leisure. It does not value traditional women's work. It does not account for environmental destruction. It assumes that consumerism is positive.

A very unequal economy in which people work very long hours and buy things to meet every need, and every whim, will have a much higher GDP than one where there are high levels of equality, where people work few hours, and where people meet their needs by making, sharing, and fixing things, avoiding waste, and having fun in ways that don't require consumption. GDP does not measure how well we are caring for each other or for our home, the Earth.

Ecological Economist's Attempts to Save GDP

While many economists who are looking into environmental questions are doing deeply transformative work, many, unfortunately, are still working with some of the worst tools of mainstream economics. Environmental economics has evolved as a subfield within the discipline of economics that uses the tools of mainstream economics to ask questions about the environmental crisis. It tends to focus on concepts such as market failure (the cases where markets don't produce good outcomes), externalities (where businesses are able to not include the full cost of their product into the price of a good, and so they "externalize" thing like pollution or child labor), and valuation (working to find ways to add the value of things like "ecosystems services" into the cost and price equations of traditional economics). Some of its practitioners promote work on better approaches to growth, such as green growth.

Bringing these and other concepts into economic analyses has allowed those working in this field to do a better job at addressing environmental concerns than those not using these tools. But ecological economists often rely on the core set of assumptions that drive mainstream economics, and so its practitioners often replicate the mistakes of mainstream economics. They tend to value growth. They tend to lean on markets as their favored way of making social decisions. And they tend to assume that low levels of governmental regulation are good for the economy.

A recent example of this approach is Per Espen Stoknes' book, *Tomorrow's Economy: A Guide to Creating Healthy Green Growth*. In that book, Stoknes offers the concept of healthy green growth as an alternative to GDP, the traditional measure of growth. Stoknes shows that after many decades where economic growth almost always led to worse impacts on the environment, very recently, some countries have begun to see a decoupling of growth and environmental impact. That is, they have GDP growth without increases in environmental destruction. Growth is not always bad for the environment, and because of that, he argues, we don't need to point our economies toward "degrowth" and take limiting growth as a goal for environmental sustainability.

Stoknes offers a tool for measuring what he sees as an unmitigated good: healthy green growth. The book develops clear, quantitative tools for aggregating GDP growth, resource productivity (a measure of how efficiently production uses natural resources), and social well-being (a measure of how much it redistributes wealth). "Healthy growth is measurable, profitable, more resource productive, and more distributive by design" than standard GDP growth.

Stoknes insists that healthy green growth is the best way to measure the health of an economic system, because growth is a positive word and we are so used to it that it sets off positive feelings in our minds when we hear it. Stoknes is in a battle on the one side against what he calls "grey growth" or simple GDP growth. On the other side, Stoknes is worried that the messages of those who want to reject growth and GDP are messages of austerity, which tell people that they must do with less. He worries that if the environmentalists abandon a commitment to growth, people will not vote for politicians who promote environmentalist policies. He is right that there is a strong tradition of austerity and doing without in environmental circles. But that critique does not apply to the people doing serious work in this area. Juliet Shor's book on the way forward is called *Plentitude: The New Economics of True Wealth*. In it she argues for a society with enough for everyone with reduced work time. We can stop using GPD as a measure of the success of an economy without asking people to have less pleasure in life.

Stoknes argues that GDP growth is a good way to fund improvements in human well-being. Like many economists, he believes that as economies have more throughput of goods and services being bought and sold, they often have more stuff and that more stuff could end up bringing people out of poverty. And so, he argues that we should look at GDP as a proxy for human well-being. And yet a few pages after making that statement, Stoknes admits that there are many places in the global south where, in recent years, GDP has grown at the same time that inequality and poverty have grown, and so the growth did not lead to increased human well-being.

Stoknes worries that without some form of growth measurement we won't have the tools we need to measure the success of our economies. But, already most national economies measure greenhouse gas emissions, inequality, and progress toward sustainable development goals. The question isn't if we should throw away GDP and not measure economic success. The question is does GDP or "growth" add anything to the mix? GDP is a useful metric for measuring the sheer output of the commercial part of an economy. Where is it used to measure the health of an economy it has the perverse incentive of making increased buying and selling into a virtue.

Measuring the Health of an Economy

There are several measures being used that capture a more complex range of socially positive outcomes that we can track to see if given policies lead to good outcomes. These new indexes do not make household labor invisible, and they don't nudge society toward wasteful consumption, and they don't favor profits over well-being. Three of the more well known of these are the Human Development Index, the Happy Planet Index, and the Genuine Progress Indicator.

The Human Development Index (HDI) tracks life expectancy, level of education, and per capita income. Because it does not account for inequality, a supplemental version was developed that factors in inequality, that version is called the Inequality-adjusted Human Development Index (IHDI). The country that most often comes out at the top of both versions of this ranking is Norway.

The HDI does not take environmental issues into consideration. To deal with the ecological implications of a countries' lifestyle, the Happy Planet Index was created as an alternative. It tracks subjective life satisfaction of a population, life-expectancy, and per-capita ecological footprint. The country that generally comes out on top of this ranking is Costa Rica.

The most well-developed of these indexes is the Genuine Progress Indicator (GPI). It takes a much more detailed approach and measures several specific economic, social, and environmental factors. It adds for positive things and subtracts for negative ones. The economic category includes measures of personal consumption expenditures and also income inequality. The ecological category includes a variety of measures including noise pollution and air pollution. The social category includes the value of household labor and the costs of crime. Because it is quite difficult to measure each of these things, and few countries have this data on hand, there are not national rankings for GPI yet. GPI has the virtue of being very comprehensive. Its use has been slowed by how complex some of its elements are to measure.

These measures have the virtue of not supposing that when more of our lives of dominated by markets, or by states, that we are better off. The insight from feminist economics, that we are better off when we have the time and resources for provisioning, and so where less of our lives are wrapped up with what it typically seen as economic processes, is well served by these indexes. For example, the GPI does not ask if a child is cared for or fed by its parents, its community, by state provided daycare, or private daycare. It simply measures if children are staying alive, eating well, and learning to read. These indexes look at the social results that would follow from good social and economic policies. They do not nudge society toward using markets to meet people's needs, as dominant economic approaches that encourage GDP growth would. Nor do they point to the state as the best provider of care. These indexes are helpful for showing the value of household labor. They are based on a broad definition of what count as economic concerns.

If everyone believes that increased GDP means a better economy, then by definition we are saying there can never be enough. But as we saw earlier, there are many reasons why GDP should not be used to measure the health of an economy. Rather, we need to shift to using economic indicators, such as the GPI, which ask deeper questions than GDP does about the state of our societies. More governments are using alternative economic indicators. The government of New Zealand no longer tracks GDP and instead uses the GPI. In 2021, Representative Ilhan Omar introduced a bill for the US government to use the GPI.

Efficiency and Markets

Mainstream economics is right that it is difficult for a society to decide how much of which things which people should have. There are not enough premium gourmet goods to meet every desire. We should all hope to live in a world where the way we eat is better than the supplies we might get in a refugee camp to meet our caloric and nutritional needs. Within constrained limits, markets can be a fine way to allocate some resources.

68 Economics Based on Scarcity and Infinite Growth

Some of us may want fancy chocolate, and be willing to pay a lot for it at the store. Others may think that it is more desirable to work less and not eat fancy chocolate.

Markets can be used to allocate some resources, in cases where there are other social mechanisms in place that guarantee that everyone has ways to access what they need. Markets work when they are embedded in strong social regulations so that we are never offered chocolate that was grown using slave labor or that required rain forests to be chopped down. If there are strong social systems in place that ensure that everyone has what they need and that ensure that people are not exploited in the process of their production, it can work well to allow some resources to be allocated by markets.

One of the most common arguments for allowing markets to be the main ways that goods are allocated is the claim that they are "efficient." What mainstream economists mean by efficiency is that when producers compete to sell things at the lowest prices, the ways things are made is pressured to be as inexpensive as possible, and this gives incentives to come up with ever cheaper ways to produce things. In this case "efficiency" means produced for the lowest possible cost. The companies that produce the most efficiently are the ones that are favored by the market. Even Karl Marx drew positive attention to the ways that capitalism helped revolutionize the ways things are produced.

But that concept of efficiency is a very narrow goal. It doesn't mean that things are produced in ways that are the most optimal for society, that the best or the most important goods are made, or that they are produced in the ways best for the environment. Things that become trash almost immediately can be produced very efficiently. It can be very efficient to pay workers as little as possible. It can be very efficient to produce things in ways that pollute, as long as the producer doesn't need to pay for that problem. Mainstream economists acknowledge that when producers don't need to pay for the hidden costs of production, such as pollution, that is a problem, and they call those cases externalities. They argue that when a cost of production is externalized there can be political decisions to make the polluter pay. But this is an extra, added on to the paradigm, and generally, politics is supposed to not interfere with the "efficiency" of the market.

The great economic historian Karl Polanyi argued that most societies in human history have had markets, where people buy and sell some things. What makes capitalism unique is the ways the logic of the market comes to dominate over other ways of deciding how to produce and allocate the things we need and want.[22] Even Adam Smith, the inventor of the idea of the invisible hand of the market, in his *Theory of Moral Sentiments*, argued that markets need to be supplemented by other forms of social decision-making.[23]

A few lessons from this:

1 Economics as a discipline needs to take seriously the values that underlie the mainstream approach. The idea that the needs of the rational maximizer should drive social decisions is a value judgment.
2 Society does not work best when markets are allowed to decide who gets what.
3 People without money have no impacts on markets. The "demand" in the concept of "the laws of supply and demand" is really "effective demand" or demand backed by money.
4 Work needs to be done to analyze the relationships between scarcity, abundance, and sufficiency.
5 Defining "the economy" as things that are bought and sold makes household labor invisible.
6 We need to stop using GDP to measure the health of an economy and switch to more comprehensive measures such as the Genuine Progress Indicator (GPI).

Notes

1 *Microeconomics*. 2022. Elumen. These are the opening lines of a microeconomics textbook. https://courses.lumenlearning.com/wm-microeconomics/chapter/understanding-economics-and-scarcity/, page 1.
2 John Ridley. 2005. "A $10,000 Martini at the Algonquin Hotel." National Public Radio Morning Edition, March 1.
3 International Student Initiative for Pluralism in Economics. 2014 open letter. http://www.isipe.net/open-letter.
4 Clair Brown. 2017. *Buddhist Economics: An Enlightened Approach to the Dismal Science*. Bloomsbury.
5 *Microeconomics*. 2022. https://courses.lumenlearning.com/wm-microeconomics/chapter/understanding-economics-and-scarcity/, page 1.
6 Paul A. Samuelson and William D. Nordhaus. 2001. *Economics* (17th Edition). McGraw-Hill, page 4.
7 George A. Akerlof. 1978. "The market for "lemons": Quality uncertainty and the market mechanism." *Uncertainty in Economics*. Academic Press, pages 235–251.
8 For current numbers of homelessness in the US, see https://usafacts.org/data/topics/people-society/poverty/public-housing/homeless-population/?msclkid=-d59717ec356c19154f72751be43cb6f3. For numbers of vacant homes in the US in 2020, see https://housegrail.com/how-many-vacant-homes-are-there-us/. For an analysis of the relationship between vacancy and homelessness, see Tanuka Loha. 2011. "Housing: It's a Wonderful Right." Amnesty International, December 21. https://blog.amnestyusa.org/us/housing-its-a-wonderful-right/.
9 Rachel Hahn. May 12, 2020. "These Moms Fought for a Home—And Started a Movement." *Vogue*. See also The Moms of Magnolia Street. https://www.youtube.com/watch?v=KZLqjTxSNVM.
10 Amartya Sen. 1982. *Poverty and Famines: An Essay on Entitlement and Deprivation*. Oxford University Press.

11 Mike Davis. 2002. *Late Victorian Holocausts: El Niño Famines and the Making of the Third World.* Verso.

12 Mike Davis. 2002. *Late Victorian Holocausts: El Niño Famines and the Making of the Third World.* Verso, pages 738–739.

13 Herman Daly. 1991. *Steady-state Economics: With New Essays.* Island Press.

14 Adel Daoud. 2011. "The modus vivendi of material simplicity: Counteracting scarcity via the deflation of wants." *Review of Social Economy,* 69.3, 275–305, 275.

15 Mary Robinson. 2019. *Climate Justice: Hope, Resilience, and the Fight for a Sustainable Future.* Bloomsbury, page 134.

16 Nancy Folbre. 2014. "The care economy in Africa: Subsistence production and unpaid care." *Journal of African Economies,* 23.suppl_1, i128–i156, i135.

17 Nancy Folbre. 2014. "The care economy in Africa: Subsistence production and unpaid care." *Journal of African Economies,* 23.suppl_1, i128–i156, i145.

18 J.K. Gibson-Graham. 2007. *A Postcapitalist Politics.* University of Minnesota Press, page 70.

19 Fred Block and Margaret Sommers. 2014. *The Power of Market Fundamentalism: Karl Polanyi's Critique.* Harvard.

20 Jenny Cameron and J.K. Gibson-Graham. 2003. "Feminising the economy: Metaphors, strategies, politics." *Gender, Place and Culture: A Journal of Feminist Geography,* 10.2, 145–157.

21 Ann Ferguson. 1989. *Blood at the Root: Motherhood, Sexuality, and Male Dominance.* Pandora, pages 77–99.

22 Karl Polanyi. 1944. *The Great Transformation.* Beacon.

23 Adam Smith. 2010. *The Theory of Moral Sentiments.* Penguin.

Chapter 5

Capitalism, Socialism, and Solidarity Economics

> It bothers me to see people lying on the street when other people are wasting money flying into space. On the other hand, it seems like if the taxes on the wealthy are too high, then there will be no innovation, and then everyone ends up poor, right?[1]

> Any time you try to move away from capitalism using elections, you end up with the business class destroying the alternative. I believe in revolution. The only reason it seems like socialism doesn't work is because the capitalist class destroys it every time. They don't want us to know that another world is possible.

> If we build enough cooperatives, then those cooperatives trade with other cooperatives, and eventually we will have a world where everyone can take care of their needs without needing any governments.

The highly polarized nature of conversations about economic systems encourages us to suppose that there is a black and white choice to be made between authoritarian socialism and free-market capitalism. Many people thinking about these issues suppose that an economy is either capitalist or socialist, as a whole. This is as true for people working in the socialist tradition as it is for people who are pro-capitalist. Many socialists argue that capitalism needs to be overthrown in a revolution and that any mixing of capitalist and socialist elements will lead to the destruction of a socialist economy.

There is an alternative anti-capitalist tradition, based in the work of Richard Wolff, Steven Resnick, and J.K. Gibson-Graham. That tradition has tried to open up our imaginations to seeing the complexity of the economic processes around us and to not accept the ways that capitalism encourages us to think about markets as the core of an economy. According to this tradition, capitalism is defined as economic processes based on private property and the private appropriation of value from workers in wage labor. Socialism is defined as economic processes that are run by a state. This tradition argues

DOI: 10.4324/9781003354871-6

72 Capitalism, Socialism, and Solidarity Economics

that there are many economic processes operating in any society at any given time.[2] In addition to capitalist market processes and state-run processes, there are also the ways we meet our needs that have nothing to do with money or government. This third category is made up of the things we make for one another, the care we give to each other, freely and voluntarily, and based on social relationships. This third aspect is often called provisioning.

If we understand capitalism, socialism, and provisioning in this way, we can start to see that almost every national economy in the world is in fact a mixed economy. It has "socialist" and "capitalist" elements in it. And as feminist economics shows us, those two are not the only sets of practices that make up an economy. Much "economic" activity is neither based on markets nor is it run by a state.

The boogeyman of authoritarian state socialism has helped keep people from being able to imagine alternatives to a rapacious and unsustainable capitalism. And yet, those are not our only two choices. Just as we need to avoid the pitfalls of capitalist approaches to economics, there are also some problems with traditional approaches to socialism that need to be taken seriously. By reifying capitalism and socialism into extreme cases to be for or against, we miss the nuance on what kinds of economic policies serve us well, and we miss seeing realistic and actionable pathways to those better economic policies.

Capitalism

Supporters of capitalism often claim that we cannot enact policies that put human and ecological needs above the pursuit of profit, because "capitalism" is the engine that has led, and will continue to lead, to a rising tide that lifts all boats. They argue that trade and growth, and letting markets make decisions about where to allocate resources, with as few regulations as possible, are fragile and will lose their magic if they are tinkered with.

The dramatic extension of average human lifespan over the course of the twentieth century is often used as evidence to support the claim that capitalism is good for human well-being. And yet, lifespans increased through the twentieth century in both nominally capitalist and nominally socialist countries. As I argue in *Getting Past Capitalism: History Vision, Hope*:

> Life spans increased in the twentieth century largely as a result of basic public health policies that included the use of sewers, clean water, and good nutrition. While in many cases an increase in capitalism has gone along with a decrease in poverty, such as the development of the Asian Tiger Economies in the second half of the twentieth century, in many other cases increases in capitalism have led to increases in poverty (such as the collapse of those same Tiger economies in the 1990's and the transition from socialism to capitalism in the Soviet Union and Eastern

Europe). In China, the transition to socialism led to dramatic decreases in poverty, as did the Chinese transition from socialism to capitalism.[3]

Mainstream economics also tells us that without the competition that capitalism creates, there will be no incentive to make better products and to make them in increasingly "efficient" ways. And yet, the capitalist way of organizing an economy incentivizes people to make things cheaply that we don't need, such as children's jewelry that has lead in it, and causes brain damage. And it puts social resources into addictive forms of social media, and crypto-currencies, rather than into cures for rare diseases. The COVID-19 vaccine was produced incredibly rapidly, largely based on the work of research teams at public institutions. That technology was given over to private corporations which did a good job with speedy manufacture. But many people died because the distribution of the vaccine was slowed as private companies asserted their intellectual property rights and did not allow cheap, generic production.

Pro-capitalist thinkers also argue that without the threat of losing one's livelihood, people will not work. And yet many people love to do meaningful work, and there are many ways to incentivize the kinds of work that are less appealing. Small levels of inequality are not particularly corrosive to the social fabric, and so in a largely egalitarian society people who do unpleasant work might get some extra bonuses or work shorter hours. Farm labor is not bad if one doesn't have to do too much of it for too long, and if it doesn't involve exposure to dangerous pesticides or exploitative management. For generations people have fought to protect their family farms. In the US, those farms have disappeared, not because no one wanted to work on them, but because corporate agribusiness made them economically unviable.

We do not need to leap into an unproven unknown new society to get rid of capitalist ways of thinking about the economy and to fight for a society less dominated by decisions made in the interests of private capital. We will be better off to the extent that we have less of each of those destructive things. A society with much lower levels of inequality and with markets shaped to meet social needs will not kill the goose that lays the golden eggs of prosperity.

Thomas Piketty has shown that in the US, the biggest era of growth in modern capitalism was under the more egalitarian phase of 1950–1980. As inequality has increased in the US in more recent decades, productivity and growth have actually decreased.[4] The monopoly-based, finance-driven, form of capitalism that is dominant in much of the world right now is bad at producing human happiness, it leads to poverty, and it is driving our environmental crises. And it turns out to even be bad for attaining the GDP growth that is the holy grail of mainstream economists.

There are quite a few societies that have achieved something close to enough, and they are not the ones with the most pro-capitalist approaches to their economies. On one side of the scale are high income countries like

Sweden, which have high taxes on wealth, and where tax money is used to provide public goods such that everyone has health care, everyone has access to quality education, everyone has access to a job, and everyone has access to housing. At the low-wealth end of the spectrum are healthy indigenous societies and nations such as Bhutan, which produce enough wealth for basic creature comforts and have strong social bonds, such that everyone is cared for and everyone has security because of the strength of those social bonds.

One of the things that happens as capitalism becomes more dominant in a society is that people are stripped of ways to take care of their needs outside of their dependence on the market, and so they become dependent on the success of capitalism to survive. Work in capitalist wage labor is alienated, meaning that people do not have control over their lives at work, and the fruits of their labor are controlled by the owners of the means or production. And, perhaps most significantly for the ecological crises we face, in a society with a strong and lightly regulated capitalist sector, those working in the interests of capitalism have tremendous power to shape how society functions.

Karl Marx argued that money is concentrated social power.[5] The companies that gain wealth through capitalist production come to work together to use that power to shape the society in which they operate. The Koch brothers in the US are one of the most important recent examples of this. Having gained wealth through a variety of businesses, including fossil fuel-based ones, the family then used their money to fund think tanks and policy organizations to fight for deregulation of the industries they owned. They also worked for broader goals to shape the context in which their businesses operated. They funded the Cato Institute and the Heritage Foundation to help spread pro-capitalist ideas and policies. They helped create the American Legislative Exchange Council (ALEC) to write laws and peddle them to legislators they helped get elected. They launched the Federalist Society to take over the judiciary in the US, to promote laws that favored their interests.[6]

While on the surface, sometimes it looks as though much of the work of right-wing politics is about "culture wars," such as fighting against women's and queer rights, or against the teaching of anti-racist history, in fact, those culture wars are only there to develop grassroots support for the policies that could never in themselves generate electoral majorities. The work of many right-wing megadonors is ultimately guided by crass material interest in shaping the political field to suit their ability to profit. Getting to a world of enough must involve taking that extreme power to shape social decisions away from the business interests that are running society in ways that are socially and environmentally destructive.

Challenging Capitalism

Many anti-capitalists suppose that the only way to end the problems generated by capitalism is to overthrow the capitalist system. The idea of a system,

Capitalism, Socialism, and Solidarity Economics 75

implied in that approach, supposes that capitalism defines the totality of a given society, and it asks us to get rid of that totality. It does not help us understand the parts of society we want to keep and build on. It supposes that we need to leap into an unknown completely different social totality to have a better world. It supposes that all of society needs to be turned upside down to get rid of capitalism. When we think of capitalism this way, it becomes hard to imagine the steps we need to take to get to a better world. What should we do while we are waiting for a revolution to happen? Should we try to make things better to build that new world? Should we try to make things worse so the system will crash?

In their book, *Half-Earth Socialism*, Troy Vitesse and Drew Pendergrass argue for an ideal sustainable society that would have indigenous controlled nature preserves on half of the planet and socialism on the other half. They offer a strong vision of what that end state might look like. The idea that half of the earth needs to be preserved for nature is gaining ground globally and was discussed in Chapter 1. The idea that we need to have socialism on the other half is less widely accepted and will be discussed below. At the beginning of the part of their book that describes how their alternative would work, they ask the reader to "imagine that the Half-Earth Socialist Revolution happens tomorrow."[7] With this move, they sidestep the question of how we get from where we are to where they want us to be. This avoidance is common among anti–capitalist thinkers, and it is related to the way they think about the nature of capitalism.

Vitesse and Pendergrass see "capitalism" as something generated by an agent they call "capital." They write, "the capitalist is not the 'master' in a capitalist society .... The master is capital itself." They are right that in a capitalist society there are processes that come to dominate that are larger than individual capitalists. For example, if the CEO of Exxon-Mobil were to decide to be a climate warrior tomorrow, he would immediately be replaced by his board. But that doesn't mean that capitalism is controlled by an agent called "capital." If capital is everywhere and nowhere and no one in particular is in control of it, it becomes very difficult to imagine what we would need to do to stop it.

Capitalism is not a system that can be thrown away, or toppled, or smashed, in any clear way. Rather, its tendrils are woven into human society in a wide variety of ways. Capitalism is perpetuated by the actions of many people at many social locations. To understand what we need to do to challenge it, we need to look carefully at the forms of agency that make our world continue to be dominated by destructive capitalist logics. Seeing "capital" as the core agent does not help us to understand those forms of agency. To get to a world of enough we need to break down the notion of capitalism into its component parts and see the different forms of agency that help it spread and the forms of agency that can be mobilized to challenge it. We need to see the aspects of our world we want to build on to develop a better world from

76 Capitalism, Socialism, and Solidarity Economics

where we are in this world. We need to challenge each form of agency that perpetuates capitalism in all of the places where we can.[8]

To return to the example of the Koch brothers, they did tremendous work to entrench fossil fuel-based capitalist processes. Doing battle to undo their work, and work like it, is a crucial part of challenging capitalism. All of the work that we do to lessen the dependencies created by capitalism help free us from its grip. All of the things we do to elect legislators who will use the power of the state to regulate in human interest, and not in the interests of capital, get closer to that ideal. All of the things we do to challenge pro-capitalist ways of understanding the world help that project. Given the ecological crises we face, these changes must be made in a short time frame and we can't wait for a revolution to put them into place.

Common ways of thinking about the nature of capitalism and anti-capitalism have limited the imaginations many generations of anti-capitalist thinkers.[9] In addition to seeing capitalism as a total system in ways that are not helpful, many anti-capitalist thinkers have very narrow views of the kinds of power that anti-capitalist organizers have at their disposal. Much of it is based on simplistic repetitions of ideas from anti-capitalist founding thinkers such as Marx.

Marx had argued that the main crux of capitalism was the extraction of value from workers on the shop floor of industrial factories. He then argued that stopping that process through strikes was a crucial anti-capitalist tactic. Marx wasn't wrong that strikes at the point of production are a useful place to challenge the power of capitalists. But his followers are wrong to suppose that strikes are the main place where anti-capitalists have power or that they are the best place to focus when solving problems not related to workplace issues.

In *Climate Change as Class War*, Matthew T. Huber correctly argues that saving the climate will require taking power from the capitalist class. To stop the forces of fossil fuel-driven capitalism, we need to understand how deeply entrenched in society those forces are. But Huber uses a narrow and outdated form of Marxism to argue that this only really happens at the point of production, where workers have their most power to disrupt the extraction of profits. His favored strategy for dealing with the climate crisis is to take over electrical workers' unions and fight from within those unions for pro-climate worker militancy that can stop fossil fuel-driven electrical systems in their tracks. His advice to young people who want to do something for the climate is to "join a union."[10]

Huber argues that the current climate movement is dominated by the professional class which focuses on discouraging consumption, and spreading the conclusions of science, to help people know what we are up against. That professional class approach supposes that knowledge itself will change society without a struggle. In contrast, Huber argues that,

> to defeat the entrenched power of the capitalist class, we will need a mass popular movement. I argue only the working class has the capacity to

Capitalism, Socialism, and Solidarity Economics   **77**

achieve this kind of mass movement. We can define the working class as those separated from the means of production and forced to sell their labor to survive.[11]

The problem with his definition is that the professional class which he is so dismissive of falls into this definition of working class, and indigenous people who are fighting for the ability to control land that capitalists are trying to take over, do not. Huber is mixing up two very different ideas here. One is his helpful analysis that many people misunderstand the nature of what we are up against with the climate crisis and suppose that it can be addressed without a power struggle. The other is the question of which kinds of tactics are needed to address the crisis. There is a tendency in the Marxist tradition to suppose that once you have identified the class of people who are the core drivers of historic change, once those people see their class interests clearly, the pathway to action becomes clear.

Generations of feminists, those organizing service sectors, and organizers from the global south have worked within the anti-capitalist tradition to displace this hundred-year-old image of the working class as the men who work in industrial labor as the core idea of the working class. Generations of thinkers have pointed out that there is no one core agent of change, and no one core place that capitalism must be challenged. Capitalist forms of destruction are generated at many social locations, and so there are many different places where those working to stop pro-capitalist forms of agency can fight against them.

Huber argues of the industrial working class that

> its strategic location at the point of production gives it structural power over the sources of capital's profits and social reproduction more generally. Working-class power is most effective in periods of mass strikes and disruption.[12]

And yet it is not clear how having a small fraction of the working class engage in strikes that disrupt the electrical system will build power and support for climate action among the part of the working class that are also consumers of electric power, or why workers in the electrical industry would be convinced to carry a broad set of demands for better forms of electricity to save the climate, over their own demands as workers.

Aside from how difficult it is for an outsider to take over an established union, Huber's view is blinded by a traditional form of Marxism that focuses narrowly on a single place to use working class power to crash the system. Huber wants us to use an orthodox Marxist view of class struggle as the core of climate action. His narrow approach misses a huge number of the tools available to transform society that are being used right now and which need to be amplified. Huber is right that successful work to save the climate will require a fight against the entrenched interests of the capitalist class. But he is wrong to suppose that the point of production of industrial profit extraction is the core place where we can fight to take away the power of those entrenched interests.

At this late date, with only a few years left to deeply de-carbonize human society, we cannot afford to focus on one narrow strategy. The urgent fight we are in, for the survival of our species, requires that we engage in all possible forms of struggle to get there. The systems that are driving us toward destruction of the climate and biosphere are deeply embedded in the fabric of society, and have tremendous resources, including the ability to use the violent powers of government, to back them up. All around the world, indigenous leaders who fight against expansion of the extractive economy are murdered for their advocacy. In many countries in the world neo-fascists have already taken over governments or are the brink of it. The powers of capitalism are entrenched at many social locations. They will not give up easily. Fighting them requires that we use everything we have.

Given the urgency of the climate crisis, and given the centrality of fossil fuel and agribusiness sectors in driving climate and habitat destruction, it makes sense to focus most directly on those sectors, as we work to rapidly build a livable world. The other crucial sector to focus on is finance, which drives many forms of destruction, and is enabling the work of the fossil fuel and agribusiness sectors. We can work to expose the campaign donations of those companies and stigmatize candidates who take it. Fossil fuel divestment is a strategy for exposing the political power of the fossil fuel industry. We can work to nationalize the dying fossil fuel industry and put its workers on the task of cleaning up the mess left at sites of extraction.

We can fight the entrenched forces of a fossil fuel-driven capitalism through protests that shut down the installation of new fossil fuel infrastructure, through street actions that shift what is politically possible, through legislation, through building alternative economic enterprises and creating thriving communities. Transnational institutions such as the IMF and World Bank, the major investment banks of the world, and many governments, are still supporting fossil fuel expansion projects. The work of those institutions needs to be challenged. Simply explaining to people our common interest in a livable world will not be enough to stop those who profit from our destruction. But neither will strike at electrical facilities.

Capitalism not a "machine." It is not a "system" that can be cut out from the social fabric in one clear way or with one narrow strategy. Rather, it is a set of ideas, and an interrelated set of practices, buttressed by entrenched forms of governmental power, which have evolved over the past five centuries. Unwinding it requires a variety of tactics and work on many fronts.

Socialism

In *Half-Earth Socialism*, Vitesse and Pendergrass define socialism as "society emancipated from the relentless, unconscious, and irrational power of capital."[13] That implies that socialism is the whole of a society that is not capitalist. Theirs is a common approach among socialists, and unfortunately it feeds a way of thinking that makes it hard to conceptualize a transition away from capitalism. It feeds the image of a society as either a capitalist whole or a socialist whole. It then encourages us to wonder how we replace one total system with a better one. Additionally, by seeing socialism as the conscious control of "the economy" it doesn't encourage us to wonder about the ways that we can shrink the aspects of our lives that exist in a separate part of the social world called "the economy" and expand the provisioning and care-based aspects of society. Another weakness of their approach to a socialist economy is that it asks for a higher level of centralized coordination than is needed, which can lead to an overconcentration of power, which we know from past socialist experiments can lead to an oppressive state.

If we step back from a totalizing way of imagining socialism, and instead think of the socialist aspects of the societies we already have, we can see that socialism has proven itself to be a very effective way to run many aspects of an economy. Under Wolff and Resnick's definition, most countries of the world already have large socialist sectors. Governments run enterprises, typically things like schools, transportation systems, health care, and safety net programs such as low-income housing. The idea that private for-profit ways of running things is more "efficient" than state-run enterprises is one of the greatest myths of pro-capitalist propaganda.

Many countries have national health care systems where market mechanisms have nothing to do with how medicine is practiced, and those systems generally have better outcomes than profit-driven medical systems. Many countries have well-run and affordable systems of public transportation which make decisions about where to put resources on the basis of need. Good systems of public transportation, run by states, are much better for meeting human and environmental needs than are systems based on private automobiles. Comparing the successes of public versus privately run charter schools in the US shows that public schools usually do a better job for children and with better working conditions for teachers. In the US, social security has proven to be a better system of old age support than the stock market-based private pensions that many pro-capitalist activists would like to replace it with. Proponents of an expansion of capitalism would have housing, health care, child care elder care, and many other aspects of our life "commodified" and turned into processes that can be bought and sold. Many of those things work much better when they are managed by well-run democratic states or when contexts are supported that enable provisioning.

80 Capitalism, Socialism, and Solidarity Economics

In addition to these examples of states creating and managing the "enterprises" that meet people's needs, there are many other things states do to take care of people's needs to create a context in which human lives can thrive. Systems of universal basic income provide people with access to what they need to survive without relying on a market in labor to have their needs met. Governments can enact environmental laws, such as regulating the use of fossil fuels, which force economic decisions on the basis of something other than a market. Governments can enact minimum wage laws and limits on work hours. They can tax wealth to increase equality. If we understand socialism to be the parts of an economy that are run by a government in the public interest, we can see that socialism has a proven track record of working.

In *Half-Earth Socialism*, Vitesse and Pendergrass argue for an ideal society in which much of the economy is run by governments using sophisticated cybernetics embedded in a democratic global governance system. They want to get rid of capitalism's unconscious way of managing society and replace it with conscious planning. In their system, markets are allowed for small things, like what kinds of food to buy, or how much clothing, or whether or not to go on vacation, but these things are limited. Vitesse and Pendergrass suggest that most of our social resources should be managed by a coordinated system of resource allocation.

They follow the work of Stafford Beer and Fernando Flores, who designed one of the first cybernetic approaches to economics that was used with some success in Chile during the presidency of Salvador Allende. Beer and Flores' system helped the government manage production as the country was being attacked by a right-wing coup that was supported by the US. Vitesse and Pendergrass are right that the parts of an economy that are run by a government should be run well and are right that sophisticated information systems can help develop smart management processes to allocate resources in ways that are useful for meeting human needs, while minimizing environmental impact.

But there is nothing new or revolutionary about using sophisticated technology to manage resources. One aspect of capitalism, which is often under recognized, is that companies operating within a capitalist context manage their internal "economic" systems without using markets.[14] They decide how much of what to buy, what kinds of resources to put where, how much of what to make when. Many companies are run using complex management systems very much like the system used to manage the state sector of the economy in Allende's Chile. Within a firm, processes need to be organized on a basis other than a capitalist market. And many of those same management principles are being used to run government sectors of many economies. Well-run systems of public transportation, education, and medical care are good examples. We already have a variety of systems in place that do a good job of managing the provisioning of resources.

Vitesse and Pendergrass suppose that their cybernetic approach to rational management of an economy should be put in place to manage resources on a global level. In *The Economics of Feasible Socialism*, Alec Nove criticized earlier forms of this idea of a centralized government-controlled economy. He argued that a centralized economy concentrates too much power into too few hands. If those decision-makers are truly accountable to the rest of society, a centrally planned economy might work. But most experiments in central planning have taken place in political systems with very low levels of accountability and little responsiveness to people's desires. And so, that concentration of power has led to corruption, bad economic decision-making, and tyranny.[15] To build an economics of enough, the transition away from capitalism needs to involve increased structures of accountability in government, and it needs to avoid, to the extent possible, concentrating power.[16]

And it turns out that there is no reason, as we move away from capitalism, to concentrate so much decision-making power in a central government. If we look at well-run systems that exist already, we can see that, where they are well run, state enterprises are often managed by a patchwork of separate entities at different levels taking care of social needs. Those systems, such as school systems, exist within overlapping sets of regulatory contexts that can hold them accountable and ensure that they meet social needs.

For example, I work in a community college district that is funded by the state, which educates thousands of people annually, at a low cost to the state and an even lower cost to students. In recent years, the state chancellor's office, at the behest of the state legislature, passed laws requiring that each district has a sustainability a plan and will, for example, only build new buildings with very high environmental standards. In this case, there is a patchwork of entities doing work that ends up with students learning green buildings. There was no one central authority that coordinated that whole dance. And different forms of governance overlap and enable things to happen without any one governmental agency having too much power on its own.

We can see the weakness in Vitesse and Pendergrass' proposal of a centralized management of the global economic system in their proposal for a global per capita limit on energy use. They promote the idea, developed by Switzerland's Federal Institute of Technology, that we should plan how societies are run based on a fair share of energy use per person in the world, and they claim that fare share would be 2,000 watts per person per year. The idea of fare shares of energy usage is helpful for analyzing the world according to how different lifestyles require different amounts of energy and to help us to look toward the ideal of equal per capita energy to judge policies and practices. This is especially helpful for reinforcing idea that many people, especially in the global south, should have higher carbon footprints than they do at present, even as the world decarbonizes.

The web page for the 2000-Watt Society says that they calculate watts based on the embodied energy in any given practice, so that, for example, if I live in a place with a very efficient system of transportation, my energy use will be lower than for someone who lives in a place with a terrible system. And yet their web page promotes personal reflection on energy use, such that when I make personal choices, I will think about my energy budget and make better choices to try to stay within my 2000 watts.[17]

This way of thinking resonates with the highly individualist approach of the carbon footprint, popularized in the 1980s by British Petroleum. By individualizing what are ultimate the results of complex social processes, it encourages us to look to the wrong places for solutions. The complex watt per person goal can be a useful concept at a very macro level to help us judge countries and regions and how they are managing. Vitesse and Pendergrass use the concept much more broadly and argue that deciding the level of per capita energy use and allocating it should be made by global central planners. They don't explain how that would be monitored or enforced. It is hard to imagine it being a good idea for a global entity to be given the authority to decide how much energy per capita should be consumed and even worse for that entity to have the power to enforce those limits.

Socialist economic processes are managed by states, and states involve tremendous concentrations of power. Anarchists raise important questions about how states come to use violence to control people. Marxists have rightly pointed out the ways that states can come to be captured by pro-capitalist interests. Those two problems lead many people to argue that we should live without states. And yet, it is hard to imagine human society that numbers in the billions without that society living in large cities, which are much more sustainable for large populations than dispersed living. And it is hard to imagine people living together in cities without there being some entity that manages the collective fabric of society.

If we define a state is a set of institutions that make decisions about how society will function over a large territory, then we should not be asking if we are for or against states. Rather we need to ask how we keep the powers that are concentrated in any system of decision-making that works over a large geographical span, accountable to the interests of those living under, or impacted by, that system.

Rather than being for or against states, or focusing on setting up an ideal state, it is more productive to think about how the powers that exist in states can be held to account. As I argue in *Challenging Power: Democracy and Accountability in a Fractured World*, we should look at democracy as a situation where power is held to account, and so people can have an impact on the institutions that impact their lives.[18] Accountability democracy is an approach to power that says that wherever there is a concentration of power, people need to constantly work to hold that power to account by developing accountability mechanisms. Accountability mechanisms work by giving

Capitalism, Socialism, and Solidarity Economics   83

voice to social concerns, getting others to see the importance of a given problem, and mobilizing social resources to limit unjust accumulations of power. There is no avoiding the necessity to be constantly vigilant about the many ways that power tends toward concentration, and there is no avoiding the need to manage the systems through which we live together.

States which are more democratic have mechanisms built into them to prevent unjust accumulations of power from taking place. They have mechanisms for translating popular interests into the state's decision-making process. They have ways of limiting the influence of money over democratic processes. They have constitutions that set a framework of basic principles for the society to follow and be bound by. They have independent and accountable judiciaries that balance the power of the majorities operating in government to check that form of power. They have mechanisms in place to keep money or cronyism from influencing decisions. Many advocates for a deeply democratic society argue for the notion of subsidiarity, where decisions get made at the lowest level possible. But some decisions need to be made at the macro level and that is where an accountable and democratic state comes in.

Solidarity Economics

An approach to building a postcapitalist world, which avoids an imagined leap to a new system based in a powerful state, is to begin where we are and to solve problems as we face them, keeping fairness, equity, sustainability, accountability, and the desire for a good life in focus. The task before us is not as grand as how to manage the needs of everyone in the world via some global mechanism.

We need to fight against the forms of agency that give power to pro-capitalist forces; work for increased democracy and accountability in our political systems; work to increase the levels of fairness in existing mechanisms for resource allocation; fight against the militarism and transnational trading systems that enforce exploitation; and change how we think about the nature of economics. We need to ensure that human needs are met, that there is enough for nature, and that people have the ability to develop satisfying lives. We need to push for policies that realize those ideals from within the reality that we inhabit. In an ideal society, some of our resource production and allocation may be managed by markets, some may be managed by a democratic state, and much will be managed by provisioning which does not take place in what has traditionally been seen as "the economy."

Solidarity economics is an emerging approach that pulls together ideas from feminist economics, as well as from the socialist and anarchist traditions. It asks how we can manage the resources of our earthly home, such that people can live well within the ecological limits of the planet. It takes seriously the need to shift toward economies more based on the provision of public goods, more based on ensuring that everyone's basic needs are met, and where we work fewer hours, and so take care of more of our needs via provisioning, outside of the realm of markets and states. Social Solidarity Economy (SSE) is a term used in much of the global south to describe this approach. People working in the English-speaking countries of the global north tend to work within the framework called New Economy.

The SSE movement has its roots in Latin America in the 1990s.[19] There are several global networks dedicated to promoting this form of economic thinking. One of the most well known is the Intercontinental Network for the Promotion of Social Solidarity Economy—RIPESS as it is known by its Spanish acronym. RIPESS came together at a meeting of representatives from over 30 countries in Lima Peru in 1997. Now, RIPPES is made up of members and networks from all around the world.

According to RIPESS,

> The Social Solidarity Economy is **an alternative to capitalism** and other authoritarian, state-dominated economic systems. **In SSE ordinary people play an active role** in shaping all of the dimensions of human life: economic, social, cultural, political, and environmental. **SSE exists in all sectors of the economy** production, finance, distribution, exchange, consumption and governance.[20]

In 2008, RIPESS published a charter, which puts forth the following values:

1 Humanism—putting human beings, their dignity, culture, and full development at the center
2 Democracy—promoting democratic values
3 Solidarity—mobilizing resources and establishing relations with other social collectives
4 Inclusiveness—establishing dialogue based on the respect for ideological differences
5 Subsidiarity—promoting grassroots development to overcome common problems
6 Diversity—encouraging representation of players of all sectors of society
7 Creativity—promoting innovation that contribute to social change
8 Sustainable Development—respecting the balance of the ecosystem by protecting the environment and biodiversity
9 Equality, equity, and justice for all—fighting against all forms of discrimination and oppression
10 Respecting the integration of countries and people—opposing economic, political, and cultural domination of the North over the South
11 A plural and solidarity-based economy—providing an alternative to the neoliberal economic model by taking actions toward a plural and solidarity-based economy[21]

The New Economy paradigm is similar, but it focuses somewhat more on small businesses and less on the informal economy. Gar Alperovitz writes,

> At the cutting edge of experimentation are the growing number of egalitarian, and often green, worker-owned cooperatives. Hundreds of "social enterprises" that use profits for environmental, social or community-serving goals are also expanding rapidly.[22]

One of the core institutions promoting new economy organizing in the US is the New Economy Network (NEN), which, according to Alperovitz, is

> a loosely organized umbrella effort comprising roughly 200 to 250 new-economy leaders and organizations, was the low-budget product of their meeting. NEN acts primarily as a clearinghouse for information and research produced by member organizations. For-profits have developed alternatives as well. There are, for example, more than 11,000 companies owned entirely or in significant part by some 13.6 million employees.[23]

In *America beyond Capitalism: Reclaiming our Wealth, Our Liberty, and Our Democracy*, Gar Alperovitz explores a wide variety of non-capitalist forms of production and distribution that are already functioning in the US. He outlines the tens of thousands of non-capitalist projects thriving in the US, from public power agencies, to worker-owned cooperatives, to employee-owned businesses. He argues that society is more fulfilling and democratic when enterprises are based around a different principle than profit maximization. In cooperatives, people have more control over the processes they experience at work.

Social Solidarity Economics and New Economics are opposed to free-market capitalism, and they are opposed to authoritarian state socialism. Those working in the New Economy school of thought often take greater pains to distance themselves from the socialist tradition than do the largely global south practitioners of Social Solidarity Economics. Some people working in these areas suppose that these alternative economic practices can develop on their own without intervention from governments. Others work to pass laws that will support the flourishing of individual projects, such as public banking support, tax breaks, and seed money to start projects. Thinkers in both traditions focus on ways to encourage local democratic activity that meets people's needs, while being ecologically sustainable. Both traditions focus on the importance of subsidiarity, where local people control their economic activity and work processes, to the extent possible. And both traditions firmly reject mainstream economics' focus on growth. Both promote the use of economic indicators that are not based on growth.

86 Capitalism, Socialism, and Solidarity Economics

One of the biggest differences between the socialist and solidarity economy traditions is that the latter take provisioning seriously. And yet, most advocates of social and solidarity economics are not opposed to also having parts of the economy run by states or markets. Solidarity economists argue for worker owned cooperatives and networks of worker owned cooperatives. They argue for strongly democratic governments, and for processes to decide democratically how to allocate capital to new projects, and to allow as much autonomy for projects as possible. They also argue for well-developed public goods, and a social provision for things like health care, housing, transportation, and education.

People working on solidarity economics look to ways to free people to take care of their needs without those needs being managed by "economic" processes. When people have enough time, they can take care of their own and other people's children and elders. They can grow a lot of food locally in gardens. They can make and fix things for themselves and for others. The provisioning aspect of a society can be very low impact in terms of the environment, and it is often the part of life where people experience the most freedom and joy.

The more time people have to live full and purposeful lives, the less tied they are to consumerism for their happiness.[24] Analysts have found that shorter work hours lead to significant drops in greenhouse gas emissions.[25] While finance capital is always looking for the place to make the most profit, governments and non-profit institutions can invest in ways that meet social needs. They can invest "patient capital" with social outcomes in mind. If we have high rates of taxation on wealth and income, we can have the money needed to invest in the things we need to live well. If we have low levels of inequality, then people are less driven to wasteful and unsatisfying consumerism and less driven to a politics based on hate and division.

Conclusion

In *Doughnut Economics: 7 Ways to Think Like a 21st-Century Economist*, Kate Raworth uses the image of a doughnut to illustrate the need to avoid poverty while staying within the planet's ecological limits. We need to find ways to keep the world producing enough stuff and distributing it in ways such that no one falls into the doughnut hole. The outer edge of the doughnut is the ecological limit, beyond which we are using so much stuff that we destroy the atmosphere around the doughnut. We need to stay on the doughnut—the sweet spot where we produce and distribute resources well. Raworth calls on economists to take that set of concerns as the core goal of their work and to develop tools to help guide policy makers to achieving those goals.

The question we need to ask about an economics of enough is: what are the practices and policies that get us to where we want to be. The serious question for economists of enough is: how can we develop the economic

Capitalism, Socialism, and Solidarity Economics 87

tools to get us to a world where we have no poverty, where our practices are environmentally sustainable, and where people feel that they are living well.

Building on Raworth's metaphor, it makes sense to look at the totality of human society and ask deep questions about whether or not current policies are meeting people's needs, and whether or not we are leaving enough for the rest of nature. We need to push for policies at every level of human society that maintain those limits, whether through transnational institutions, national governments, or as a result of grassroots pressure to enforce those limits. And we need to then allow for as much of a free flourishing of human life as possible within the limits imposed by the outside of the doughnut. An economics of enough needs to take the elimination of extreme poverty and environmental sustainability as two bedrock limits for any economic policy. Chapter 6 looks at how we stay within those limits.

A few lessons from this:

1 It is helpful to think of countries as having a variety of economic processes happening at the same time, rather than being "capitalist" or "socialist" as a whole.
2 It is possible to challenge the capitalist aspects of a society without taking a leap into an unknown new social formation all at once.
3 If we define socialism as economic processes managed by a government, we can see that most economies of the world have socialist sectors, and in many cases those sectors are run better than when those sectors are run according to capitalist principles.
4 Economic activity that is neither controlled by markets nor controlled by states can be some of the most satisfying and ecologically friendly ways to take care of our needs. Policies can be promoted to help social and solidarity economies thrive.
5 Economists need to take up the challenge of guiding social policies toward ensuring that everyone has enough while respecting the limits imposed by a healthy ecosystem.

Notes

1 These statements, when they don't have a separate footnote, are made up and are intended to represent the kinds of things people say on the subject of the chapter.
2 Stephen A. Resnick and Richard D. Wolff. 1987. *Knowledge and Class: A Marxian Critique of Political Economy.* University of Chicago Press.
3 Cynthia Kaufman. 2012. *Getting Past Capitalism: History, Vision, Hope.* Lexington Books, page 30. For a study of the causes of lifespan increases in the twentieth century overall, see: Jim Ueppen and James W. Vaupel. 2003. "Broken Limits to Life Expectancy." *Science's Compass Policy Forum.* http://www.soc.upenn.edu/courses/2003/spring/soc621_iliana/readings/oepp02b.pdf.

4 Thomas Piketty. 2021. *Capital and Ideology*. Harvard, page 24.

5 Karl Marx. 1978. "'The power of money in bourgeois society.' Economic and philosophical manuscripts of 1844." In Robert C. Tucker, ed. *The Marx-Engels Reader*. W.W. Norton, page 101.

6 See: Jane Mayer. 2017. *Dark Money: The Hidden History of the Billionaires behind the Rise of the Radical Right*. Anchor; Nancy MacLean. 2018. *Democracy in Chains: The Deep History of the Radical Right's Stealth Plan for America*. Penguin.

7 Troy Vettese and Drew Pendergrass. 2022. *Half-Earth Socialism: A Plan to Save the Future from Extinction, Climate Change and Pandemics*. Verso Books, page 117.

8 This is the core argument of Cynthia Kaufman. 2012. *Getting Past Capitalism: History, Vision, Hope*. Lexington Books.

9 J. K. Gibson-Graham. 1993. *Waiting for the Revolution, or How to Smash Capitalism while Working at Home in Your Spare Time*. In *Rethinking Marxism*, 6.2, 10–24.

10 Matthew T. Huber. 2022. *Climate Change as Class War: Building Socialism on a Warming Planet*. Verso, page 281.

11 Matthew T. Huber. 2022. *Climate Change as Class War: Building Socialism on a Warming Planet*. Verso, page 6.

12 Matthew T. Huber. 2022. *Climate Change as Class War: Building Socialism on a Warming Planet*. Verso, page 6.

13 Troy Vettese and Drew Pendergrass. 2022. *Half-Earth Socialism: A Plan to Save the Future from Extinction, Climate Change and Pandemics*. Verso Books, page 150.

14 Leigh Phillips and Michal Rozworski. 2019. *The People's Republic of Walmart: How the World's Biggest Corporations Are Laying the Foundation for Socialism*. Jacobin.

15 Alec Nove. 1991. *The Economics of Feasible Socialism Revisited*. Cambridge University Press, page 120.

16 Cynthia Kaufman. 2020. *Challenging Power: Democracy and Accountability in a Fractured World*. Bloomsbury.

17 2000 Watt Society. https://www.2000-watt-society.org/.

18 Cynthia Kaufman. 2020. *Challenging Power: Democracy and Accountability in a Fractured World*. Bloomsbury.

19 Peter Utting. 2015. Social and Solidarity Economy: Beyond the Fringe. Zed Books.

20 http://www.ripess.org/what-is-sse/what-is-social-solidarity-economy/?lang=en.

21 http://www.ripess.org/what-is-sse/what-is-social-solidarity-economy/?lang=en.

22 Gar Alperovitz. 2011. "The New-Economy Movement: A growing group of activists and socially responsible companies are rethinking business as usual." *The Nation*, May 25, 2011.

23 Gar Alperovitz. 2011. "The New-Economy Movement: A growing group of activists and socially responsible companies are rethinking business as usual." *The Nation*, May 25, 2011.

24 Juliet Schor. 2008. *The Overworked American: The Unexpected Decline of Leisure*. Basic books.

25 David Rosnick and Mark Weisbrot. 2007. "Are shorter work hours better for the environment?" *International Journal of Health Services*, 37.3, 405–417.

Chapter 6

Eliminating Extreme Poverty and Developing an Economics for Enough

> Many countries in the world have had impressive growth rates in the past few years. Just imagine with all of that business activity, how much better off people will be.[1]
>
> While you are telling us we need to engage in "good governance," your knee is on our throats. You are extracting profits based on tax fraud, manipulated prices, and predatory loans. Every time we put someone in power who is committed to bettering the lives of our people, that person if overthrown by someone in a nice suit who speaks your political language and does your bidding, and who invariably ends up being a crook. Yes, good governance is a good idea.
>
> Imagine a world where economists focused on analyzing how well we were doing in feeding people and protecting the planet. Imagine that they had tools to use that helped them to understand the dynamics that lead to well-being and ecological responsibility. Imagine that the press that covered economics looked at labor and environment and not just at how well businesses and the stock market were doing.

In a world where every year, enough food is produced to feed everyone well, many people are chronically malnourished. In the US, where houses have doubled in size in the past decades, more than half a million people don't have homes on any given night. We don't have poverty because there isn't enough. We have poverty because of the ways our resources are allocated. This is true on a global scale. The world produces enough for everyone already. The question for eliminating poverty is how to find mechanisms to produce and allocate resources such that everyone has their basic needs met. This chapter begins with a look at the causes and solutions to the problem of extreme poverty. It ends with a look at how we can live well without destroying our physical environment, and how to orient our economies toward a sense of abundance.

DOI: 10.4324/9781003354871-7

Eliminating Extreme Poverty

In 2015 the United Nations set out 17 sustainable development goals to achieve by 2030. They include things like universal literacy and access to clean energy. Goal number 1 is to eliminate poverty. Before the COVID-19 pandemic, there was much talk among the world elite that this goal was on track to being achieved, and a narrative was developing which argued that poverty was being eliminated as a result of increased global trade. It was true in that period that the number of people living on less than $1.90 per day, the bar for extreme poverty set by the United Nations, had been cut in half between 1990 and 2020. But a closer look shows that these gains were incredibly small and not enough to eliminate poverty by 2030. And, in contrast to the dominant pro-trade narrative, the gains that were made were the result of targeted poverty elimination programs, not trade.

While global commercial output has doubled since 1990, in 2019, there were 736 million people living on less than the $1.90 per day. And the halving of people living below it turns out to not mean that very much progress has been made, given what is possible. According to Paul Edward and Andy Sumner, if the bar were raised to $2.00 per day, then 100 million more people are in poverty, and so in a piece written in 2020 they argued,

> The richest decile of the population captured 39.1% of the consumption growth increment from 1990–2012, and had just 1.4% of that increment been redirected to the $2-per-day poor, they would still be left with a huge 37.7% share. This modest amount of redistribution of growth could have been achieved with fairly minor tax and transfer adjustments.[2]

In other words, a very small level of redistribution would completely eliminate extreme poverty.

As mentioned in Chapter 1, Philip Alston, the UN official in charge of leading the UN's Sustainable Development Goals project, argues that poverty is a political choice. There is plenty in the world to meet the needs of everyone.[3] Extreme poverty can be eliminated by simply closing tax loopholes and redistributing that wealth to the poor.

And yet the mainstream view, dominant in institutions such as the World Bank and IMF, is that the way to eliminate poverty is to stimulate more economic growth. As the metaphor goes: growth is the rising tide that can lift all boats. And yet, in a study for the World Bank, Christopher Lanker and his co-authors did an analysis of the impact of growth on poverty versus the impact of inequality reduction. They found that

> When holding within-country inequality unchanged and letting GDP per capita grow according to International Monetary Fund forecasts, the simulations suggest that the number of extreme poor (living

below $1.90/day) will remain above 550 million in 2030, resulting in a global extreme poverty rate of extreme poverty rate of 6.5 percent. If the Gini index [of inequality] in each country decreases by 1 percent per year, the global poverty rate could reduce to around 5.4 percent in 2030, equivalent to 100 million fewer people living in extreme poverty. Reducing each country's Gini index by 1 percent per year has a larger impact on global poverty than increasing each country's annual growth 1 percentage point above the forecasts, suggesting an important role for inequality on the path to eliminating extreme poverty.[4]

Reducing inequality has a much bigger impact on poverty reduction than does economic growth. And, as a recent Oxfam report argues, global inequality has reached the point where the "world's billionaires have more wealth than 4.6 billion people."[5] The focus on growth as a way to eliminate poverty feeds the very machine of production and consumption that is destroying environment and leading to lives of insatiability, while not solving the problem of poverty.

It is very convenient for the wealthy of the world to focus on the halving of extreme poverty as defined by living on $1.90 a day to legitimize their approach to the world economy. Many proponents of the economic growth approach to poverty elimination have touted a graph developed by Max Rosser which shows that poverty has gone down from 94% in 1890 to 10% in 2015. That seems like an astounding accomplishment, until you realize that in 1890 a much larger percentage of the population lived off the land without using money to meet their needs.

Jason Hickel writes:

> What Rosser's numbers actually reveal is that the world went from a situation where most of humanity had no need of money at all to one where today most of humanity struggles to survive on extremely small amounts of money. The graph casts this as a decline in poverty, but in reality, what was going on was a process of dispossession that bulldozed people into the capitalist labor system.[6]

In addition to these problems with measuring poverty based on the line of $1.90, much global poverty exists in wealthy countries where it is impossible to live on $1.90 a day. A much more promising approach to measuring poverty is found in the other metric used by the United Nations: The Multidimensional Poverty Index (MPI). That index measures poverty based on deprivation of basic things needed to have a decent life. It looks at specific basic needs: nutrition, child survival, years of schooling, school attendance, cooking fuel, sanitation, drinking water, electricity, housing, and assets. According to its analysis: 1.3 billion people are "multidimensionally poor."

And it breaks countries into regions and finds for example that one region in Uganda has a 96.3% rate of poverty and another region has a 6% rate.[7]

In 2020, Sabine Alkire, one of the developers of the MPI, wrote that there were signs of progress in reducing multidimensional poverty over the five-year period the tool was first out:

> Comparing the trends for multidimensional poverty and the better-known metric of income poverty helps us reach a better understanding of poverty. ...Proactive social policy either by government or other actors was often evident in countries reducing MPI. In Sao Tome and Principe, the incidence of multidimensional poverty went down, but monetary poverty actually increased during this period of zero growth.[8]

Poverty is reduced when more people have what they need to live well. As Alston argues, poverty is a political choice. The way to eliminate it is to get needed resources into the hands of those who need them. That requires challenging current systems of social reproduction that give those resources to those who don't need them. To do the political work change how societies allocate resources. How we go about that political work is the subject of Chapter 7.

Ending Poverty in the Global South

In the wealthy countries of the world, the way out of poverty is fairly intuitively obvious. A few Northern European countries have virtually eliminated poverty through high levels of taxation, low levels of inequality, and strong safety nets. Many countries in the world have enough resources to invest in providing for people if they chose to, without requiring any major transformation of how their governments and economies function. Eliminating poverty is conceptually, if not politically, a simple question of mustering the political will for redistribution and developing public goods.

In the countries of the global south, the question is much more complicated. Most of the global south was ravaged by colonialism, and transnational institutions have worked to keep processes in place that make it very difficult for those countries to meet the needs of their populations. Much of the discussion of eliminating poverty in the global south that comes from the global north focuses on good governance. And it is true that many global south countries suffer from government officials that are able to amass great fortunes for themselves, and where money for socially and environmentally destructive government sponsored projects goes to their cronies. But it is also true that, in many of these countries, leaders have been kept in place because institutions of the global north preferred those corrupt autocrats and kleptocrats to leaders who would run a county in the interest of the well-being of their people.

One infamous case was the murder of Patrice Lumumba, president of Zaire (what is now the Democratic Republic of the Congo), by the former colonial power Belgium, with support from CIA of the US. The West put Mobutu Sese Seko in power and kept him there for decades, as he looted $8 Billion from the national treasury.

That process, of Western powers putting autocrats into power and helping them stay there, has not stopped. José Zelaya was elected president of Honduras in 2006, and as he began to develop strong relationships with left wing Latin American governments, he was overthrown in a coup in 2009. Secretary of State Hilary Clinton, at the behest of President Obama, quickly recognized, and gave legitimacy to, the corrupt leaders who overthrew that elected president. Not long after that coup, environmental activist Berta Cáceres was murdered by agents of a mining company, whose operations her organization was getting in the way of.

Since that time, many Hondurans have tried to flee a country devastated by climate produced droughts, and ravaged by violence, as a result of bad governance and poverty. With a stunningly tin ear to the responsibilities of history, in 2021, during a visit to Honduras, Vice President Kamala Harris said she had one message for would-be migrants from Central America "do not come." In 2022 Xiomara Castro, the wife of Zelaya, was elected as president as a result of a wave of grassroots organizing. Also in 2022, Berta Cáceres' murderers were convicted. Good governance is indeed a good idea.

Anti-corruption measures are crucial for good governance anywhere in the world. And yet reformers tend to focus on the corruption of a given leader in a global south country, rather than on the processes that put that person in place, or the network of relationships, often based on the global north, which enable that corruption. Writing about attempts to clean up corruption in Africa, Frits Nghiishililwa writes that

> owners of foreign banks in which stolen billions of monies was deposited were not regarded as being corrupt. Neither are the leaders of the host country in which the recipient banks were located. This is a double standard. A holistic approach should be found to combat corruption not only for example, to expose and punish the corrupt African leader but also those who encourage and benefit from corrupt deals.[9]

In recent years, more attention has been put on the system of tax havens that siphon wealth from around the globe and deposit it into unregulated bank accounts. This tax haven system has its core in companies rooted in the global north, and they are supported and enabled by global north dominated institutions and governments.

Governments of the global south are also constrained in eliminating poverty by their dependence on institutions such as the World Bank and IMF. Those institutions were set up after World War II, ostensibly to help eliminate poverty. And yet they have from their beginnings been run in ways that favor the interests of global capital. Both institutions continue to pressure leaders, desperate for support, to cut back on social services and education and invest in road building and other forms of infrastructure that promote "economic growth." These forces prevent countries from developing economic systems that would serve their populations' needs. As of this writing, both institutions continue to promote fossil fuel infrastructure projects that are harmful for the climate. According to Frits Nghiishililwa,

> Conditions that have served global capital at the expense of the countries have been removal of import/export barriers, financial liberalization, currency devaluation, lower corporate taxation, export-oriented industrial policy, austere fiscal policy (especially aimed at social spending) and monetarism in central banking.[10]

Many countries in the global south find themselves with high levels of debt to these transnational institutions, as a result of years of living under these dependent relationships. They are also suffering from devastating impacts from climate change, even though they have produced only a small fraction of global emissions. In recent years, the countries of the global south have been insisting at the international climate negotiations that they get payments to help them develop sustainable economies and deal with the impacts of climate change. Wealthy countries have pledged $100 Billion a year, most of it in the form of loans, to the poor countries of the world to help them adapt to the climate crisis. And yet the global north has come nowhere near meeting that obligation. And it is not as though they cannot afford the money. They are still subsidizing fossil fuel industry at a rate of several trillion per year.[11]

A campaign called Debt for Climate, initiated by activists in the global south, is calling for cancelling the debt of poor countries in exchange for stopping the extraction of fossil fuels and developing sustainable economies. The campaign website states:

> **Developed countries of the global north owe an ecological debt to the countries of the global south. In addition to being responsible for the highest historical emissions of greenhouse gases, their exploitation and colonization of most of the global south still continues today through their multinational corporations with the systematic plundering of natural resources.** According to scientific studies, 100 multinationals are responsible for 71% of global industrial emissions. A large part of these emissions is a consequence of the exploitation of the South, fueling a system of unsustainable consumption

and waste in privileged classes of rich countries at the cost of the growing destruction and sacrifice of populations in countries of the global south.[12]

Eliminating poverty in the global south begins with honest accounting of poverty using the MDI. It also involves a change in the global political system whereby elections that bring to power leaders who are committed to bettering lives of their people are respected. It involves ending support from global north countries for corrupt leaders. It involves global institutions cracking down on corruption and tax avoidance, in all places around the world that enable those forms of corruption. And finally, it involves dramatic shifts in global financial flows, such that the global south no longer subsidizes the global north though corrupt practices. It involves the countries of the north making good on their promises to finance climate mitigation.

A fair and well-regulated transnational system would enable countries of the global south to solve their own political problems through social movements and democratic elections, without being hamstrung at every turn by transnational institutions which speak in patronizing terms about "aid" but which produce conditions that make sustainable economies just about impossible.

We need to take the elimination of poverty to be a bedrock goal of our thinking about the economy. The most important thing those studying economics can do to help us understand poverty is to look at the kinds of policies that reduce multidimensional measures of poverty. If we want to get to a world of enough, the other core goal we need to keep in our vision is sustainability. As Raworth argues, to goal of economics should be to keep us out of the doughnut hole that is poverty, and out of the air around the doughnut, which is overuse of resources.

Ecological Economics

Sustainability is the core concept used by those wanting to ensure that we do not use too many resources. Their goal is to find ways to meet our needs that do not destroy the fabric of the natural processes in which economic activity takes place. Sustainability means that the actions we take in the present do not destroy the possibility of a thriving future. Most definitions of sustainability include social as well as ecological factors and point to a future with a thriving human society that meets everyone's need while not destroying its ecological substrate. Economists such as Nicholas Georgescu-Roegen and Herman Daly did crucial early work developing an approach to economics that put the concept of sustainability as its core.

Unlike mainstream economists, who like to suppose that their work is value free, ecological economists accept that putting sustainability as the core of their work is based on a value judgment. Economic processes should be geared toward helping us to work in harmony with all of the biophysical processes that exist in nature, and they should be geared toward leading to good human lives within those limits. E.F. Schumacher's 1973 book, *Small Is Beautiful: A Study of Economics as If People Mattered*, was an early popular contribution to this tradition. It focused on the low impact, high happiness, lifestyles of many villages in the global south. He called his work Buddhist economics and argues for a principle of "enoughness."[13]

Ecological economists tend to follow the precautionary principle which says that policies should always keep in mind the possibility of unintended consequences and should err note side of caution. They argue, for example, that we do not adopt a new technology, such as genetically modified food, until it is proven safe. Ecological economists tend to avoid typical mainstream economic tools such as cost benefit analysis, that work by putting prices on natural processes. Whereas a mainstream economic analysis might argue that the economic value of a stand of trees is worth more when harvested than it offers in economic value to the indigenous people living in a forest. A broader analysis might argue that the destruction of the way of life of forest dwellers cannot have a price put on it.[14]

For them, economics needs to understand the impacts of human activity on air, land, oceans, and biodiversity. They, and their contemporary followers, argue that an analysis of an economic system always needs to carefully analyze the cycles of biophysical processes that the economy takes place in. Anyone analyzing an economic system needs to look, not just at the present and the prices of resources, but also at the impacts of the use of those resources on the systems in which they are embedded, and also at the long-term impacts of a given policy.

Mainstream economics is based on a linear way of thinking and promotes linear economic processes. Analysis begins with the "inputs to production," the raw material that are bought then looks at the process of production, then ends with the sale of the product. A company must decide if it will make a profit by manufacturing in a particular way. If it can make a profit, within the legal constraints it is operating under, then it should make the product that way. If there are not regulatory processes in place, then it is usually in the interest of a manufacturer to produce using the cheapest labor possible and to not worry about the waste and pollution it generates.

Many places in the world are experimenting with ideas of circular economies, where producers are responsible for the environmental impacts of their goods, this includes putting the carbon impacts into the price of the good, making the producer pay for those impacts, and making them responsible for recycling the goods at the end of their lives. Right now, it is in the interest of phone manufacturers to have us buy a new phone every year or so and to have the rare earth metals that were mined at so much human an environmental cost be thrown into garbage dumps. As we shift away from economic policies that encourage wasteful uses of resources, government regulations will be increasingly important. Economists need to attend to the cycles of impact that are generated by production and they need to help us develop mechanisms to ensure that the crucial biophysical substrate of our lives is protected.

What Is an Economy for?

Mainstream economics asks us to base economic policy on maximizing utility, increasing GDP, pareto optimality, and "efficiency." These concepts are deeply value laden, and the values they are based on are terrible for all three parts of pursuing a world of enough: elimination of poverty, staying within our ecological limits, and increasing happiness.

They are bad for eliminating poverty because they put the needs of the billionaire for a new home on the same level as housing for person who has no shelter. They call for allocating goods on the basis of effective demand, that is, demand backed by money, above real human needs. They arbitrarily limit our policy options to those which favor capital. And they measure the health of an economy based on how much is produced for the market, rather than on how well people's needs are met.

These values are bad for the environment because they promote buying and selling as inherently good. They promote as more productive people buying shoddy can openers that last for a year and buying a new one every year, over a system that would produce high-quality long-lasting can openers that would last for 40 years. It also gives huge levels of social decision-making to powerful companies which get governments to serve their interests rather than the interests of human society. And those values nudge all of us onto a hedonic treadmill, which encourages us to pursue consumption for status and so to allocate resources to places where they are wasted.

This approach is bad for our happiness, even for those with enough material resources to be comfortable. By encouraging high levels of inequality, low levels of social security, and a culture of competitive individualism, it encourages status anxiety in everyone, it encourages a politics of othering to create electoral majorities to support policies that only serve the wealthy and makes people unhappy with what they have.

The goal of economics needs to be reconceptualized as the study of ways to manage our resources to lead to good lives for everyone within the biophysical limits of the planet. In the social sciences, when someone claims to be value natural, they are generally hiding their value commitments. It isn't possible to develop an economic theory that doesn't have values embedded in it somewhere. What more honest approaches to social sciences do is to take their value commitments seriously, make them explicit, and allow part of the work of the discipline be an open, thoughtful dialogue over those values. The social science can then do careful, and sometimes quantitative, analysis on the basis of those well-evaluated starting points. Economics needs to develop as a discipline in dialogue with other disciplines, and with a set of values that are made explicit and argued over in the open. It needs to let go of the claim that it is a value-free science.

An economics that is mindful of its value commitments should be as agnostic as it can be on questions of how people should live and what they should pursue in life. Many of those working in the field of happiness economics try to look at what people themselves say makes them happy. Economics doesn't need to interfere too much in questions of how people want to live. It can develop with a simple commitment to the values required for enough: environmental sustainability, respect for human rights, and increased happiness for people to the extent possible.

Conclusion

The world has enough. We have the technical and social knowledge to ensure that everyone in the world has enough stuff to meet their material needs for comfort, health, and happiness, while staying within the ecological boundaries required for a healthy ecosystem. In societies with low levels of inequality, there is enough for everyone to feel successful, respected, and satisfied. Those thinking about economics, or how we manage our earthly home, need to free their minds from the shackles imposed by the 150 years of pro-capitalist propaganda that are embedded in mainstream economic theory. They need to ask deep questions about what they are trying achieve with the tools their discipline offers them. They need to take seriously the value-based assumptions that their mathematical analyses rest on. They need to learn a new set of tools that are helpful for building a world of enough.

Some of the most important things we need to advocate for to get to a world of enough, are shorter work hours, support for caregiving labor, support for public goods, decreases in the levels of inequality, and the use of alternative economic indicators. There are economic dependency traps created by capitalist processes that we need to work against to make it possible to build an economy that meets our human and ecological needs.[15] The stronger our safety nets are, with things like national health care, pensions, free public transportation, and free public education, the more we are able to meet our needs without depending on a job in wage labor. If no one's well-being is dependent on finding a job, then we don't need to buy more things in order to help people have jobs. It is possible to meet all of our material needs for comfort and well-being with everyone working 24-hour work weeks, especially as the world economy moves toward more automation. A guaranteed income, in the form of sending checks to people, or in the form of tax credits, is a good way to make sure everyone has enough to live well.

As we will see in Chapter 7, we can work to achieving each of these things through organizing and mobilizing popular pressure. We can move to increase the parts of our economies that are based on provisioning, decrease the power of private capital over our political systems, decrease the aspects of our economies that are controlled by private capital, decrease our dependencies on private capital, and increase the quality and quantity of high-quality public goods provided by states.

A few lessons from this:

1 We solve the problem of poverty when our social systems get resources to people who need them.
2 Economic growth does not in itself reduce poverty.
3 To solve the problem of poverty in the global south, the institutions controlled by the global north need to end predatory lending practices, end tax avoidance of companies in the global north, and stop supporting dictators.
4 Countries of the global north need to support democratic political processes in the global south.
5 Economic decisions need to take the three core criteria of enough into consideration: environmental sustainability, respect for human rights, and increased happiness for everyone.
6 No one should have unlimited wealth while others don't have what is needed for sufficiency.
7 Sustainability needs to be a core goal of any economic thinking.
8 The economy needs to be understood as an aspect of a deeply interrelated social world. Economic thinking needs to take culture, history, values, and politics seriously. Economic thinking needs to take place in healthy dialogue with other disciplines, with questions of values taken seriously.

Notes

1 These statements, when they don't have a separate footnote, are made up and are intended to represent the kinds of things people say on the subject of the chapter.
2 Peter Edward and Andy Sumner. 2020. "The End of Poverty and the Politics of Measurement and Governance of Growth." *Global Policy.* July 15. https://www.globalpolicyjournal.com/blog/15/07/2020/end-poverty-politics-measurement-and-governance-growth.
3 Philip Alston. "The Parlous State of Poverty Eradication." Human Rights Council. July 2, 2020, page 19.
4 Christoph Lakner, et al. 2019. "How Much Does Reducing Inequality Matter for Global Poverty." World Bank Working Paper 8869, page 1.
5 Oxfam. 2020. "World's Billionaires Have More Wealth Than 4.6 Billion People." January 20.
6 Jason Kickel. 2019. "Bill Gates Says Poverty Is Decreasing. He Couldn't Be More Wrong." January 29. https://www.theguardian.com/commentisfree/2019/jan/29/bill-gates-davos-global-poverty-infographic-neoliberal.
7 "Global Multidimensional Poverty Index 2019: Illuminating Inequalities." http://hdr.undp.org/sites/default/files/mpi_2019_publication.pdf, page 1.

8 Sabina Alkire. 2020. "How Has Global Multi-dimensional Poverty Changed over the First Ten Years of Measurement?" *Business Fights Poverty*, July 28. https://businessfightspoverty.org/articles/how-has-global-multi-dimensional-poverty-changed-over-the-first-ten-years-of-measurement/.

9 Frits Nghiishililwa. 2021. "Why Poverty Persists in Developing Countries, especially in Africa: A Case of Institutional Failure or Poor Leadership." In Nhemachena, Artwell, Tapiwa Victor Warikandwa, and Howard Tafara Chitimira. "Global Jurisprudential Apartheid in the Emergent One World Government." *Global Jurisprudential Apartheid in the Twenty-First Century: Universalism and Particularism in International Law*, Lexington Books, pages 343–368, 363.

10 Frits Nghiishililwa. 2021."Why Poverty Persists in Developing Countries, especially in Africa: A Case of Institutional Failure or Poor Leadership." In Nhemachena, Artwell, Tapiwa Victor Warikandwa, and Howard Tafara Chitimira. "Global Jurisprudential Apartheid in the Emergent One World Government." *Global Jurisprudential Apartheid in the Twenty-First Century: Universalism and Particularism in International Law*, Lexington Books, pages 343–368, 355.

11 Guardian. 2021. Editorial. "The Climate Crisis Is Just Another Form of Global Oppression by the Rih World." November 5. https://www.theguardian.com/commentisfree/2021/nov/05/the-climate-crisis-is-just-another-form-of-global-oppression-by-the-rich-world.

12 https://debtforclimate.org/.

13 E.F. Schumacker. 1973. *Small Is Beautiful: A Study of Economics as If People Mattered*. Harper Collins. For a recent work on Buddhism and economics, see Clair Brown. 2017. *Buddhist Economics: An Enlightened Approach to the Dismal Science*. Bloomsbury Publishing USA.

14 Vandana Shiva. 2005. *Earth Democracy: Justice, Sustainability and Peace*. Zed Books.

15 Cynthia Kaufman. 2012. *Getting Past Capitalism: History, Vision, Hope*. Lexington Books, page 81.

Chapter 7

Policies and Politics to Get to a World of Enough

> "First, they ignore you. Then they ridicule you. And then they attack you and want to burn you. And then they build monuments to you."[1]

In 2012 I worked with a group of students on California's Proposition 30 which raised taxes, mostly on the very wealthy, to pay for funding for education. My union hired interns to do some of the work. Many of those interns were also getting training in the community organizing program I work in.

Many of us working on Proposition 30 were excited to raise funds for schools and even more excited to be working to transform the dominant narrative that raising taxes to fund public goods was a waste of money. We didn't know at the time that we were working at an early stage of a sea change in public attitudes. That period brought with it a renewed understanding of the value of public goods, a willingness to challenge inequality, and a willingness to tax the wealthy to support those public goods. The passage of Proposition 30 was part of the beginning of a move to rebuild our educational system, decrease inequality, and develop a society that works for all.

Most of my students have grown up low income in the Silicon Valley where the tech titans generate billions of dollars in wealth. And yet, it is a place where that wealth has mostly been harmful to lower income people in the valley. The companies attract highly paid workers from other regions and communities. And it attracts tremendous amount of global finance capital to its housing market. That has raised the cost of housing to the highest in the country. Families with children are leaving the area at alarming rates. Very few well-paid jobs in tech are open to students from working-class backgrounds. Tech companies often fill their lower-level positions using subcontractors who pay starvation wages and fight against unionization. The Silicon Valley has some of the highest levels of inequality in the country and an incredibly underfunded public sector. San José, the main city in the valley,

DOI: 10.4324/9781003354871-8

has a severely underfunded bus service, poorly paved roads, underfunded libraries, and poorly funded education.

De Anza College, where I teach, is in the small town of Cupertino, just west of San José. Cupertino is the home of two large institutions: Apple and De Anza College. De Anza College educates around 20,000 students a year and is funded almost entirely from state taxes. Between 2008 and 2012, De Anza College lost 8% of its faculty and had to cut 1,000 classes per year. Its neighbor, Apple, is one of the most profitable corporations in the world. And yet Apple has managed to avoid paying billions in taxes by pretending that its profits are made elsewhere. While De Anza was laying off faculty and cutting classes, Apple had a corporate office in Reno, Nevada that allowed it to avoid paying state taxes in California. The corporate tax rate at the time was 8.84% in California and 0% in Nevada.

When the possibility came for our students to work on enacting a policy that would tax the wealthy to pay for education, many were excited to get involved. As our students come to learn about why their communities are so devastated, and as they come to feel that they had a voice and could make a difference, many of them become passionate to get involved with policy change work. Our program gives them the tools and support they need to advocate for policies that will transform the conditions under which they, and their families, live.

Students were involved in every phase of work to pass Proposition 30. They helped get it on the ballot. They registered people to vote. They educated their communities about why they should vote for it. They worked to get-out-the-vote up until the polls were closed. And finally, on November 6, 2012, they celebrated a sweet victory. Since that time, Proposition 30 has raised around seven billion dollars per year for education in California. At De Anza College, that has meant a program for free tuition, more counselors and mental health support, and more sections of the hard-to-get-into classes that are part of a great education.

The fight for Proposition 30 can be seen as one part of the beginning of the end of the Reagan Revolution, which began in California in 1978. In that year, California had passed the notorious Proposition 13, which was the opening bell of a nationwide race to lower taxes on the wealthy and starve the public sector. The Reagan Revolution was based on the ideas that government spending was wasteful and that taxation involves unfairly taking money from people who deserve it and giving it to people who don't. That story of who does and does not deserve public funding is often explicitly, and more often implicitly, racist.[2] Proposition 13 moved California from having the best educational system in the country to having one of the worst. The Reagan Revolution dominated the country for almost 40 years and was key for leading the US to having extreme levels of inequality, a starved public sphere, an overworked population, and a politics dominated by racist dog-whistles.

The work our students did to pass Proposition 30 helped to decrease inequality in California and it helped fund our starved public sector. Those are two of the core areas of policy change that are required to get to a world of enough. Reducing inequality is crucial because as we saw in Chapter 2, high levels of inequality are a strong driver of a variety social problems. Societies with more inequality have higher levels of social discord, worse health outcomes, higher levels of incarceration, and higher levels of stress. Inequality drives status anxiety, and status anxiety drives a sense of insatiability, which is part of what leads to unhappiness and wasteful consumption. And inequality leads to divisive politics.

Everywhere we turn there are opportunities to build a world of enough. There are organizations to join, and there is work one can do on one's own to support those initiatives. There is also work to be done shifting the culture in ways that move us toward a world of enough. Every one of us has the capacity to be part of the transition to a world of enough, and we will only get there if a lot of people do that work. This chapter focuses on some of the most significant areas of work needed to build a world of enough, and it looks at ways to be involved with that work.

Social Movements

Those interested in significant social change often imagine that going out into the streets is the only way to make it happen. In reality, social change happens in movements that play out over time, and those street actions are just the most visible part of a given movement. In his book *Doing Democracy: The MAP Model for Organizing Social Movements*, Bill Moyer argues that social movements go through a variety of stages, from the early stages where a small group of people begin to see things differently, to the phase when public action is taken, to the phase where ideas come to be institutionalized in laws and policies. People on the outside are often dismissive of those doing work at an early phase of a movement, rejecting it as unrealistic. It often is too visionary for the current moment and so others sometimes see it as counterproductive, because it can create a negative response in the mainstream.[3] But that early radical envisioning is crucial of opening up our imaginations to new ways of being, and building a small core of people to do the work.

Then there is the middle period where visible actions become larger and people begin to have to think about the issues raised by the movement, and public opinion begins to shift. Only after a lot of contesting does the view that seemed marginal gradually gain cultural acceptance.

There is a time late in a moment when its ideas begin to gain acceptance. Moyer describes this phase in most social movements where the street actions fade and many people who have been involved think the movement failed, because it is no longer the center of everyone's attention. Moyer calls this phase "perception of failure." He argues that this is the time where the movement's largest gains are possible. But the key movers shift from those who are rebels on the street, to the inside players who negotiate with legislatures to enshrine the new public understanding into new laws and policies.[4] After a movement has captured the public's imagination, the stage is set for gaining legal rights and a shift takes place from being ignored, to persecution, to acceptance, to real lasting systemic change.

One well-known and classic example was the civil rights movement in the US. It began in very quiet ways in the 1940s and over the next few decades peaked. At first those pushing for voting rights for Black people in the South were met with violence and division, and very few people though that the situation could ever change. There were few activists and the forces they were up against were deeply entrenched and there were few early victories. Over time more small skirmishes happened and the number of people who joined the movement grew.

At its peak of fame, the movement engaged in dramatic actions, such as sit-ins and boycotts, that captured the public's attention. At that point people not involved in either fighting for or against civil rights had to form an active opinion on the situation—they needed to take sides. As the actions escalated, the movement gained support. One of the most brilliant strategic moves of the civil rights movement of that period was that it adopted mainstream dominant values of "liberty and justice for all" and engaged in non-violent civil disobedience to expose the oppressive power of pro-segregationist local governments to television cameras. The conjunction of those two aspects of the movement helped turn the white majority in the country away from support for segregation. The movement said to the country, "we were just sitting down having lunch in a peaceful manner, hoping to be treated with equality, and these people are attacking us with dogs."

Not all movements are committed to nonviolent civil disobedience, more aggressive forms of disruption can also galvanize attention and force policy makers to act. In the late 1960s many people in the cities of the North began to insist on racial equality. And in many cases riots broke out. Those too galvanized national attention and told the country that something needed to change. Those more disruptive movements take a different approach to galvanizing public opinion, but they go through the same series of phases. They are not trying to gain sympathy, rather they work by getting those in power to understand that a change must be made for there to be the social stability they desire.[5]

When people think of social movements, they generally think about the phase of open contestation where the movement is on the streets. But those street actions cannot happen without a lot of hard work, forming organizations, developing ways of understanding issues, and developing strategies and messaging within the nascent movement. And they would not have much social impact if they didn't engage in the later phase of the movement, where the movement shifts from the streets to popular culture and to the legislature, where laws and policies are changed.

Political scientists use the concept of the Overton window to describe the range of political opinions on any given topic that are considered reasonable, and therefore actionable, by the mainstream at any given moment. Street actions are one of the most consequential things organizers can do to shift the Overton window on a given subject. That shift opens opportunities for institutionalizing lasting change, but they don't constitute lasting change themselves.

There are a few lessons to be learned from Moyer's analysis. One is that social movements require different forms of action at different times. Different people are attracted to different forms of action, some like to be outsiders on the street and others like to be insiders walking the halls of the legislature. Often in movements people attracted to one form of action don't respect the work of people who do different forms, but movements work best when there is synergy between the different approaches.

Another insight from Moyer's work is that social movements take a very long time. An action is not a movement. Movements only make lasting change when a society's values and beliefs change and those changes become deeply woven into the social fabric. Those sorts of changes take a lot of work over a long period of time. And movements rarely solve a problem once and for all. Rather, a cycle of action can solve some part of a social problem, but generally deeply entrenched social problems take many cycles over many periods of time to truly be resolved.

With the civil rights movement, we can see Moyer's cycle being repeated over and over again. The movement that peaked in the 1960s led to tremendous changes in US society. And it left many forms of racism in place. It was followed, as a form of backlash, by a devastating increase in incarceration and a continued brutal policing of Black communities. The more recent movement against police violence that drew people onto the streets after the brutal murder of George Floyd is, as I write this, now still percolating through our institutions. In Santa Clara County, California where I work, there is a slow and complex set of organizing happening to keep the county from building a new jail. That work, which is not taking place on the streets, was made possible by the shift in perception unleashed by the street actions that took place in 2020.

In *From Twitter to Teargas*, Zeynep Tufecki argues that social media makes the mobilizing part of a social movement much easier than it has been in previous times. It is now fairly easy to advertise an event, and it is easier for an event to get attention once it happens. In her analysis of the Gezi Park occupation in Istanbul Türkiye, which she was involved in, she makes that case that social media made the movement able to grow quickly and peak with minimal and relatively unformed organizational structures behind them. An unfortunate result of that was that activists were not able to translate the shift in public opinion they created into lasting social reforms. That next phase of achieving institutional reforms required a group who could engage those with power and negotiate concessions.

Moyer's cycle only really works, as he describes, in countries that have at least partially democratic legislatures. In the case of an authoritarian country, the street action could lead to a political crisis and an overthrowing of a regime, but again, if there is not sufficient organizational structure in place to take advantage of that situation, and if the system the movement is confronting is not open to the possibility of reform, then the energy unleashed by the movement cannot be captured and translated into lasting structural change. In authoritarian countries social movements may lead to repression or revolution, but almost never reform.

Moyer's model makes movements seem more linear than they are, and yet the general view of how social change happens that emerges from his work is very helpful. Movements often start with a small group seeing world differently, their view grows and action happens to make people take notice and think about the issues, and then opportunities open for changes to be institutionalized. Often on any given issue, there are a few phases of operation at one time, and not all movements need to hit the streets to make progress. Though generally if you are fighting entrenched interests that have something to gain from society not changing, you are going to need to do a lot to overcome the power of those entrenched interests. In community organizing, people talk about the power that comes from money, the power that comes from people working together, and the power that comes from disruption.

We are at a moment in world history here the climate crisis makes it impossible for us to continue business as usual. If we keep emitting greenhouse gasses at the present rate, then much of the planet will become uninhabitable. And yet deeply entrenched forces are fighting to the death to keep us from transitioning to a path of sustainability. They are already murdering environmental activists in the global south. They are spending billions of dollars fighting lawsuits and supporting politicians who are keeping us on a path to destruction. They have already succeeded in undermining the fabric of many societies with the culture wars they unleash to gain electoral majorities. The forces committed to the continued burning of fossil fuels are like sociopaths, who only care about their own success and have no social conscience. Stopping them will take all of the organizing skills we have.[6]

Policy Change

Policies are the rules and laws under which our common world operates, and large-scale changes that begin with impossible seeming ideas can eventually get adopted and institutionalized. There is a dynamic relationship between an individual sense of right and wrong, and how things should be in our common world, the values that we share about how we should act, and the rules under which we live. One slogan from community organizing is that "rules and laws are power frozen in time." The struggles we have over how the world should be end up crystalized in the laws and rules that govern society. Rules change when there are politicians changing them, and they tend to make those changes in response to the people to whom they are accountable. Sometimes they change rules because their constituents ask them nicely to do so. Sometimes they change rules because their wealthy donors ask them to. Sometimes they change rules to keep riots from breaking out. Whether the relations between a rule maker and those pressuring them is based on chummy inside relationship such as lobbying, or it is based on fear of all hell breaking loose, either way, there is a dynamic relationship between rule makers and the rest of society.

Policy change is not work for someone else. All of us can be involved in making policy change happen. We can work to elect politicians who support our ideas. We can join social movements that pressure politicians to enact the policies we believe in and shift the Overton window. And policies can happen at all levels. Sometimes important policies are started in a small town where they are tried out before they become state, national, or transnational initiatives. The next sections look at some of the most important areas to work in to build a world of enough: reducing inequality, supporting public goods, shifting cultures, and reducing the economic dependency trap of capitalism.

Reducing Inequality

As we saw in Chapter 2, a strong driver of wasteful and unsatisfying consumption is status anxiety. The single biggest driver of status anxiety is inequality. Getting to a world of enough will require us to focus on the hard policy work of shifting how societies distribute resources. As Pickett and Wilkinson argue in *The Spirit Level: Why Great Equality Makes Societies Stronger*, some societies achieve low levels of inequality through progressive taxation, but some, such as Japan, have achieved fairly low levels of inequality by making sure that the gaps between high and low wage workers are not great.[7] It doesn't really matter how we get there, but societies that are able to enact policies that keep inequality to a relatively low level are ones with much higher levels of happiness, lower levels of poverty, and smaller ecological footprints.

In the history of modern capitalist societies, there have been a wide range of levels of inequality. In the US, the gilded age at the end of the nineteenth century and the second gilded age, which is the present, have been characterized by extremely high levels of inequality. In both periods, the rich were allowed to get richer through low levels of taxation, lax rules on monopoly concentration, political systems captured by the very wealthy, and weak labor movements. The first gilded age ended with the reforms fought for by the progressive movement, the rise of a powerful labor movement, and finally with the policies of the New Deal. Those policies led to what is often described as the post-war prosperity, a period of relative gains in living standards among white people. While there were also gains for people of color, those gains were smaller because many of the policies of the New Deal were exclusionary, such as the rules governing agricultural and domestic labor, and the rules governing who could access government guaranteed home loans, and because many labor unions excluded people of color.[8]

Globally, countries with strong labor movements have generally achieved relatively high levels of equality. In Cuba, the revolution of 1950 led to a communist government that has kept economic inequality to a minimum. The tiny country of Bhutan is run by an authoritarian monarchy, which also ensures minimum standards of living and works to ensure a high general level of well-being for the population. The social democratic counties of northern Europe are well-known examples of places with high levels of equality, strong public sectors, and strongly democratic traditions. Those countries moved toward equality as results of powerful and disruptive labor movements, early in the twentieth century. The tiny Central American country of Costa Rica had a powerful and rebellious leftist movement that engaged in strikes and other actions and led to a constitution in 1948 that abolished the military and guaranteed economic rights.

If we see that unequal societies have been transformed in the past, we can see that it is possible for us to do it again in the present. Our current gilded age in the US is ripe for a challenge to inequality. Many politicians and social movements are working to regulate monopolies, close down tax havens, and reform the tax code to tax the rich and corporations. One of the first acts of the incoming Biden presidency in 2021 was to give an earned income tax credit to low-income families. This move singlehandedly put millions of people on a pathway out of poverty. For the short period it was in place, it cut the child poverty rate in half.

Movements that have led to nationwide transformations in inequality have generally come as the result of years of organizing and have needed to be massive, and often unruly, to achieve their results. Entrenched powers will do all they can to prevent these sorts of changes, and the more money and power a sector of society has, the harder it fights to keep its privileges. None of the policies argued for in this section are easy to achieve, and yet none are pipe dreams either. All have been tried and won, and lost again, and won again over time. There is no pathway to a world of enough that doesn't include the hard and disruptive work of challenging relations of power.

Tax the Rich

The most obvious policy tool for lessening inequality is changes to systems of taxation. Anyone can join an organization that is working to build support for taxing inequality out of our systems. There is a wide variety of ways to

Policies and Politics to Get to a World of Enough   109

tax the rich. Very high marginal income taxes, capital gains taxes, taxes on wealth, and estate taxes are all helpful. Equally important are aggressively chasing after tax havens and a wide variety of forms of tax fraud which are widely tolerated at the present time.

Wealth Tax

When she was running for president in 2020, US Senator Elizabeth Warren argued for a wealth tax of $2 per million on the top 0.1% of households. She argued that such a tax would raise trillions of dollars to support public goods and that it would have a minimal impact on the wealthy individuals who paid it. According to her web page:

> The Ultra-Millionaire Tax taxes the wealth of the richest Americans. It applies only to households with a net worth of $50 million or more— roughly the wealthiest 75,000 households, or the top 0.1%. Households would pay an annual 2% tax on every dollar of net worth above $50 million and a 6% tax on every dollar of net worth above $1 billion. Because wealth is so concentrated, **this small tax on roughly 75,000 households will bring in $3.75 trillion in revenue over a ten-year period.**[9]

While Warren's plan focused on the money that such a tax can bring in to public coffers to support public goods, in his run, in that same race, Senator Bernie Sanders went a step further and argued for wealth taxes that would eliminate the billionaire class entirely. In addition to wanting to raise funds for public goods, Sanders argued that because of the ways that wealth impacts our political system, we would all be better off in a society without billionaires. Sanders' interest in the wealth tax is also motived by the need to redistribute that wealth downward, so that the rest of society can have the fair share needed to live good lives. He argued that his proposal would:

- Establish an annual tax on the extreme wealth of the top 0.1 percent of US households.
- Only apply to net worth of over $32 million and anyone who has a net worth of less than $32 million would not see their taxes go up at all under this plan.
- Raise an estimated $4.35 trillion over the next decade and cut the wealth of billionaires in half over 15 years, which would substantially break up the concentration of wealth and power of this small privileged class.
- Ensure that the wealthy are not able to evade the tax by implementing strong enforcement policies.[10]

Both Sanders' and Warren's proposals would have helped to bring us to levels of inequality we had in the US in the very prosperous period 1950–1980.

110 Policies and Politics to Get to a World of Enough

Neither discussed the psychological impact of lessening inequality, but both of their proposals would have been powerful steps toward a world of enough. By decreasing inequality and using the money generated from a wealth tax to pay for social goods, and distributing wealth downwards, they would have had the benefits of lessening poverty, supporting public goods, and also decreasing the status anxiety that drives consumerism.

Many people argue that wealth taxes are not the best approach because several countries in Europe enacted them in the period 2008–2015 and ended up rolling them back after a few years' time. And yet studies of the impacts of wealth taxes have shown them to be very effective at raising revenue and decreasing inequality. Because they tend to hit the top 0.1%, even in the capitalist sectors of an economy, they have no negative impact on entrepreneurship and innovation in the economy. In fact, they are likely to have a positive impact, since the extremely wealthy tend to use their power to squash the entrepreneurship of those below them on the economic ladder.[11] In places where they were enacted and then withdrawn, they were withdrawn because of enormous political pressure from the wealthy.

There are a few things that need to be in place for a wealth tax to work. It needs to cover all asset classes, so a wealthy individual can't use loopholes to shift their wealth from one type of holding to another to avoid the tax. The government would need to invest significant resources into going after people who try to cheat on it. The government enacting them needs to be able to withstand the political pressure from the very rich. Where these conditions exist, wealth taxes have been incredibly successful.[12]

Transaction Taxes

One of the most dangerous aspects of the present global economic reality is the rising power of finance capital. An older model of capitalism had people gaining wealth from having workers make things and selling them at a profit. The newer model has investors seeking gains through less productive means. People profit from speculating on changes in stock prices, from buying companies on the hopes that they will increase in value, by buying companies and stripping their assets for short-term profits, and increasingly, from buying homes and leaving them empty. As finance capital is increasingly freed to search for short-term profits, with little regulation, and few requirements that it do anything to support the productive economy, the economies of the world are being hollowed out and turned into places from which wealth is simply extracted. In the older version of capitalism wealth was extracted but goods and services were produced along the way as a by-product.[13]

Much of the profits in the stock markets of the world are made with high-speed trading intended to profit off of infinitesimal differences in stock prices. These high-speed trades do nothing to provide capital to help businesses grow or to make useful products. Instead, they are a way to make profits without engaging at all with the productive aspects of the economy. Many people have proposed small taxes on stock transactions to raise money for social goods and to discourage the unproductive and dangerous games of high-speed trading. Economist James Tobin proposed a tax on short-term buying and selling of currency as a way to discourage currency speculation. The idea of a Tobin tax has since broadened to include any taxes on short-term speculative transactions in order to raise funds for public goods and to discourage speculation.

Income Tax

Throughout the twentieth century, and into the twenty-first, income taxes have been one of the most common ways to raise money for governments to fund public goods. When they are highly progressive, they can help diminish inequality. Trump's tax reform made the income tax in the US much less progressive, as the top 0.1% percent of households reaped 60% of the benefits, and where many middle-class taxpayers in large Democratic states saw their taxes go up. In my lifetime, whenever the Republicans have enacted a "tax cut," my taxes, as a low and then middle-income person, have gone up.

One of Joe Biden's first acts as president was to enact an earned income tax credit, which uses the tax system to provide something like a guaranteed income. The tax system pays money to people who made too little to actually pay taxes. While many people have argued for a guaranteed basic income (GBI), as a way to provide a safety net for the poor, Senator Bernie Sanders has argued that an earned income tax credit accomplishes much the same thing with existing mechanisms. Income taxes are a well-tested way redistribute income downward.

Estate Tax

From 1919 through 1976 there were relatively high taxes on the estates of the top 7% of most wealthy people in the country. In 1976, reforms led to sharp decreases in the level of estate and gift taxes. By 1986 only 0.3% paid any of these taxes.[14] As of 2015, only around 7,000 families paid estate taxes in the US.[15] Advocates for the very wealthy have continually fought against high levels of estate taxes, and at the present, the highest levels are only 40%, and most wealthy people find ways to shield their assets from it through a variety of tax avoidance mechanisms. Still, well-designed estate taxes have proved effective at decreasing inequality.

Developing Public Goods

Investing in public goods is a crucial strategy for building a world of enough. In a society with strong public goods, there is broad and equal access to the things people need to survive. Public goods create social solidarity. And they

112   Policies and Politics to Get to a World of Enough

make people less dependent on a job to survive. For Adam Smith, the lighthouse was the perfect example of a public good. Everyone can use it a no one can be excluded from using it. For him, and for mainstream economists, a public good is something that one person's use doesn't take anything away from. For them, lighthouses and sidewalks are public goods, but schools and public transportation are not.

Anatole Anton encourages a broader use of the term "public goods." For him they are things that are "commonstock," that everyone has a right to use.[16] Similarly, Nancy Holmstrom defines public goods as "goods for all or most of us" that can be "satisfied for one only if they are satisfied for others." She gives as examples "a close community, a clean environment, a pleasant and efficiently organized city, a park, adequate medical care system, or a good educational system."[17] For Holmstrom and Anton, public goods are broadly defined as those things that belong to the public and increase human welfare. They can be provided by the government, as in the example of public schools; they can be protected by the government, as in the example of clean air; and they can be created freely by people, as in the example of strong communities. Public goods create the social fabric that facilitates a good life.

We are often told that markets are the most efficient way to allocate society's resources. But in many cases, funding public goods turns out to be a better way of allocating resources than markets. Some communities have developed tool libraries, where people can use a tool on the rare occasion when they need one, rather than buying them and having them sit unused most of the time. A tool library is a highly efficient way of allocating tools. Public bus systems are mostly funded through taxes. They are able to make decisions about what services to offer based on a mission to serve the community. A system might decide to run buses at very early hours when few people ride, even if it isn't "cost effective," because the people who do ride at that time need that service. That might not make financial sense, but it makes social sense for there to be some way to get people to the grocery store to stock shelves before the store opens. Markets allocate resources based on who can pay. Public goods are allocated based on an analysis of what the needs are. With public goods, a democratic society can make thoughtful decisions about what kinds of policies will meet people's needs.

Investing in public goods is a way to ensure that people's social needs are met without them needing to buy things. In a society with well-functioning public goods, people are less reliant on a job in wage labor to meet their needs. They don't need a job to get access to public schools, health care, and retirement systems. In a society with good public parks people don't need yards to connect with nature. In a society with good libraries, people don't need to buy as many books. In a society with free broadband, people don't need to pay for access to what is in many places a crucial form of communication.

Adequate public transportation systems are helpful for the environment, for increasing equity, and for building stronger communities. In a society with great public transportation there is less traffic. Less space needs to be given over to roads and parking spaces. More can be used for things like open space. There is less air pollution. Cars no longer are a core status symbol. There is less of a gap between the transportation modes of rich and poor. Public goods, such as public transportation, increase equity because the things needed for a good life are available to everyone. A society with strong public goods has higher levels of happiness, more environmental sustainability, and less poverty.

Community colleges are a powerful example of a public good. The state taxes people, and those tax moneys go to pay for the colleges. Most students pay little or no tuition. Even for students who pay full tuition, the price of a student's education does not come close to the cost of that education. The taxpayers of the state pay for it because society has made a political decision that having low-cost accessible higher education serves a large set of individual and social needs. Community colleges help people realize their dreams, they increase their social mobility, they prepare them to participate in the civic life of their societies, and they prepare them for the workforce.

In addition to the argument that states should not offer public goods because markets are better at allocating resources, the other argument that is usually made against funding public goods is that "we can't afford it." And yet in the US, in 2019, military spending accounted for 53% of discretionary spending. The war in Afghanistan, which lasted for 20 years, cost thousands of US and Afghan lives and cost trillions of dollars in military spending. Human societies have the resources to meet everyone's needs. When someone makes the argument that something cannot be afforded, they are saying that they prefer resources to go to something else. In highly unequal societies, there is a very easy, and socially useful place to go to get funding for public goods: taxing the wealthy. As we have seen, forms of taxation that decrease inequality have a wide variety of benefits, including generating funds to pay for public goods.

Societies with high levels of inequality generally have underfunded public goods. Money that could go to fund public goods instead stays in the pockets of the wealthy. Unequal societies generally have low levels of social solidarity across lines of class and race. In such a society it is hard to get people to pay to educate other people's children, especially if those children are of a different race than their own. There are many states in the US where the elderly population is predominantly white, and the children are predominantly people of color. In those states, it is very difficult to raise taxes to pay for education.[18] Challenging racism is a crucial part of generating support for public goods.

Racism and Inequality

Some of the deepest forms of inequality in the US are generated through racial discrimination, from housing segregation, to the ways banks loan money, to the ways that education is funded. Fighting against inequality involves fighting for a fair distribution of the wealth of society along racial lines. Racism, or on many countries, ethnonationalism, creates a vicious cycle, where inequality becomes embedded in the social fabric, and where beliefs that justify that inequality perpetuate more inequality.

Since its beginnings in slavery and colonialism, capitalism has relied for its functioning on the dehumanization of large sectors of the population. And for a few centuries, racism and ethnonationalism have helped ruling classes create common cause with lower class members of dominant groups to uphold elite serving economic policies.

In *The Sum of Us: What Racism Costs Everyone and How We Can Prosper Together*, Heather McGee tells the story of how, when segregation was outlawed in the US, public swimming pools in small towns all across the country closed. Many white people preferred to have no swimming pool at all to sharing one with Blacks. And while that left many working class whites without a pool, wealthier whites often had private pools.[19]

Once a social system is in place where some people gain power on the basis of dehumanizing others, those benefiting from the arrangement will continue to perpetuate the ideas that keep it functioning. Some people are turned into "others" who are left outside the circle of people who matter to the dominant society, and that helps increase the sense of belonging for those inside the circle. Those who have developed their identity based on the system telling them that they are superior to others, come to be invested in preserving that system of meaning and identity, even if it does not meet their material needs. Members of the dominant group come to identify with the elites of their society as a way of distancing themselves from those despised "others."

In a society structured such that some people are seen as "others" who do not fully belong, it is difficult to form the political unity required to advocate for policies that serve society as a whole. In societies with strong racial or ethnic divisions, it is very hard to develop support for public goods, like public swimming pools and public education. Challenging racism is central to building a world of enough.

And according to john a. powell, much of that work need to focus on culture. He argues that

> a cultural strategy for belonging shifts whose knowledge and vision is made actionable in reshaping society. This grows the cultural power of those dehumanized and delegitimated towards the creation of insistently human belonging, justice, and liberation. Valuing oneself, one's culture,

and one's community, even in the face of violent negation and devaluation, is at the core of a cultural strategy for belonging.[20]

In a divided society, even though it is in the material interest of most people to advocate for public goods, the politics of race get in the way of achieving those goals. In many countries in the world right now, there are ethno-nationalist movements of the majority group that stoke a sense of othering and belonging, and that mobilize mass passions to keep exploitative systems in place. Much of the work of getting to a world of enough involves shifting the systems of meaning that make people vulnerable to the politics of racial and ethnic division.

Shifting Systems of Meaning

According to Moyer's framework, deep social change often starts with a small group of people who have a different vision for how society should be run. That view is usually ignored, and then mocked for being outside the realm of the reasonable. But, over time, many social movements succeed in realizing their visions. According to Antonio Gramsci ideas are a crucial part of the work of social change. He uses the term hegemony to describe a way on understanding the world that makes the world make sense in a way that privileges those in power. An example of this would be the ways that many people suppose that people in poverty have done something wrong and deserve their condition and so do not deserve social policies that give them access to resources as a right. Widespread acceptance of that view helps take away support for policies that would eliminate poverty.

Gramsci argued that an important part of social change was to create counter-hegemonies, ways of understanding the world that help us to see the injustice in dominant social systems, that allow us to imagine a better world, and that help us see the pathways to that better world. A counterhegemonic view of poverty says that there are unjust social forces that create poverty and that there is enough for everyone. A crucial part of social change work is generating alternative stories about our social world and making those stories appealing and popular.

The Zapatistas in southern Mexico did amazing cultural work in the late 1990s and early 2000s helping those interested in social justice to see that "another world is possible." They put out an inspiring vision of a "world where many worlds fit." Their slogans, and the idea that it was possible to build a world free from exploitation, became touchstones for social justice moments in many parts of the world, and helped to expand many people's sense of what was possible for human society.

Work done to assert the centrality of the needs and cultures of people in communities that have been dehumanized is some of the most important

116 Policies and Politics to Get to a World of Enough

work that can be done to challenge systems of domination. john a. powell writes that

> when a dominant group of people wants to subordinate or control another group, one of the first things they do is try to take away peoples' language, their religion, their food—in other words, their culture. And they work to enforce that of the dominant culture as the "norm."[21]

When people who live under a system of domination come to hold a positive view of themselves and others in their culture, when they are able to express their humanity, joy, and sense of entitlement to the resources of society, they are able to advocate for those needs and for society to change. Evan Bisell argues that challenging discourses of othering are crucial parts of a larger strategy for social change. That kind of cultural work opens up space for policy change:

> Research shows that a voter's inactivity is rooted in how they view themselves in the world and their ability to have impact through voting or other forms of civic engagement. In other words, a person's worldview shapes their interpretation of voting as an act in which they will participate or not.[22]

When the dominant systems of meaning tell people that they don't matter, when those systems tell people in the dominant group that they are special because of the ways that others have been dehumanized, you have a society that is ripe for elite control. In many places in the world, elite interests use "culture wars" to consolidate power. Stigmatized "others" are paraded as destroying the social fabric of the nation, panics are created around their ways of being. Movements for equal rights are opposed on the basis of the ways that they supposedly destroy the "normal" society for the dominant majority.

In the US, many white people have a sense of themselves as the normal regular people who matter in our society. When they feel that their centrality is questioned, many feel a sense of panic. That panic makes them vulnerable to demagoguery. Right-wing parties then create electoral support based on pushing these panic buttons and are able to build support for economic and social policies that otherwise would not have much support. The organizations in the US that are pushing battles over how race is taught in schools and whether or not children are ought to respect LGBT people are funded by wealthy donors with broader economic agendas.

Fighting against that well-funded agenda requires that we work to create alternative systems of meaning, ways of understanding the world that has room for everyone to matter. Bisell writes that,

> A cultural strategy for belonging builds upon alternative and liberatory forms of culture that people have developed before and within the

dominant cultures of capitalism, white supremacy, settler colonialism, and other forms of oppression. These cultural practices and knowledge form through people loving and thriving, resisting and negotiating, acting spontaneously and keeping continuity, engaging ritual, tending memory, and experiencing grief and joy.[23]

Cultural systems are the matrix in which we live our everyday lives, they are the water in which we swim. Many cultural activists create and share meaning in ways that help make the world make sense of our common humanity, they help us make sense of the systems of domination we are up against, and they can help point the ways to a more viable future. Cultural activism takes many forms, from creating formal works of art, such as movies and books, to informal meaning creation such as how we speak to one another and live our lives.

The Economic Dependency Trap of Capitalism

There are ways that as a society comes to be more dominated by capitalist practices, people come to be increasingly dependent on capitalism doing well. If our retirement savings are in the stock market, then we need there to be high stock prices. If our health care comes from our job, then we need for there to be a high level of employment. If our children can only go to college if we have a lot of money, then we will need a high paying job, and we will want businesses to be strong. In such a situation, people are encouraged to consume more so that more people can be employed. In a society that has more of its economy wrapped up in capitalist process of buying and selling labor, and where markets control more of the allocation of goods and services, people are more dependent on working in wage labor to get their needs met. Part of building a world of enough is to decrease the power of these economic dependency traps of capitalism, whereby people's survival becomes dependent on how well capitalists are doing.[24]

In a society with well-developed public goods, people are less dependent on their job for survival, they can downshift to part time work if they prefer it. In a society with a strong public health care system, they can more easily leave jobs they don't like without worrying about losing health care. If a person doesn't need to worry about how to afford to send their children to college or how to survive in their old age, because college and old age income come to everyone regardless of ability to pay, they are less tied to wage labor to survive. One of the most pernicious arguments for consumerism in a capitalist society is that we all need to buy things so that others can have jobs.

We decrease the economic dependency trap of capitalism by developing other ways for people to meet their needs. One of the most important ways to decrease the economic dependency trap of capitalism is the provision of

118 Policies and Politics to Get to a World of Enough

public goods. Other important mechanisms are work-time reduction, public banking, and the provision of a guaranteed basic income.

Work-Time Reduction

If people need to work 60 hours a week to survive, then they have very little time to spend on things that build community and a sense of well-being. They are stressed in terms of the time they can spend with family. They have little time to devote to civic projects, like participating in their children's schools or local politics. They generally are not as happy as people who have time to devote to the things they enjoy. It is easy to imagine that human happiness was greatly increased when work hours were reduced from 12-hour days to 8-hour days in many places in the early part of the twentieth century. It is not so hard to imagine the changes that would happen if the next step was to move toward reducing the standard work week from 40 hours toward 20. Work-time reduction helps minimize the economic dependency trap of capitalism because as people work fewer hours, jobs are able to be shared more widely, and people have more time to invest in aspects of life not related to buying and selling.

There are huge social benefits that come from people having long vacations, plenty of sick leave, and time off for having children. One benefit is there is less stress in balancing work life and home life. There is more time to take care of children and elders. Because women tend to do more of that caregiving work than men, work-time reduction can have especially positive impacts on women's lives.[25] With less time at work there is more time to be creative and take care of ones needs outside the market, via provisioning. Many of the things that come from reduced work hours lead to stronger community ties, and where there are stronger communities, people are generally happier. Happiness can come from making food and eating it with people, enjoying nature, playing sports and music, and making art.

If everyone were to work 20 hours a week, then there would be more jobs to go around for other people. This will be increasingly important as jobs become rarer in the future. It helps get off the treadmill of people needing to buy things to make sure there are jobs for people, as many jobs become unnecessary. As we make the transition to a sustainable society, if we share resources properly, then there can be enough for everyone with fewer and fewer hours spent in wage labor.

There are a few policies that are gaining traction right now that can lead to reduced work time. The most significant one is raising the minimum wage, which, at the lower ends of the pay scale, allows people to work only one job to survive. Another policy is to fighting against the manipulations of the gig economy, where workers are treated as contractors, and so not eligible for the benefits of full-time employment that the labor movement fought for and gained throughout the twentieth century. Finally, labor laws can be changed to define a full-time job as something less than 40 hours a week.

Some businesses have voluntarily moved from 40-hour weeks to 35-hour weeks and they have found that productivity does not go down. It turns out that when people are happier and have time to take care of their personal needs, they actually work harder in the time they are at their jobs.[26] France instituted a 35-hour work week in 2000. Companies were given tax credits to cover losses that they might experience. We can all fight in our local municipalities and at the state and federal levels for better laws to regulate the gig economy, for increasing the minimum wage, and for reduced work hours.

Public Banking and MMT

If investments are made solely on the basis of what is likely to give a private investor the highest returns, we will remain in the treadmill of useless consumerism and the production of disposable goods. There is no reason that investment based on private profit seeking needs to be the main form of investment in society. Governments can also invest in making the things we need to live well.

Advocates are working to set up public banks in many states in the US. For most states, when they build roads, schools, or other public goods, they borrow money from private banks and have to pay interest on those loans. Under pressure from the powerful progressive movement, in 1919 the state of North Dakota set up a public bank, which is still thriving. The state uses the money that sits in its accounts to invest in projects. That example shows that there is no good reason for a state government to pay interest to private banks for its projects. States can lend from their own coffers.

Advocates of strong public spending have also argued that there are ways we misunderstand the nature of money that led us to being fooled into believing that public spending is bad for us. In the US, when the government spends money, it is not the same things as when a household spends money. Stephanie Kelton is one of the leading thinkers of Modern Money Theory (MMT). In her book *The Deficit Myth: Modern Monetary Theory and the Birth of the People's Economy*, she argues that because the US can print as much money as it likes, there is never a shortage of money. What limits the size of an economy is the number of people who can be brought into the economy to work. Money is a form of lubricant for transactions. It can facilitate the projects that mobilize labor to engage in productive activity. Those who argue that the government should not spend too much are basing their arguments on a mistaken view of the nature of money. There is never a shortage of money if you can print more.

The economists who refute this idea generally argue that government spending leads to an economy overheating and that if we keep spending until we have full employment, we will end up with inflation, where there is so much money in the system that it loses value. Advocates of MMT agree that at there is a point at which there can be too much money in a system. But for them that point is only after we have full employment.

In the early part of the twentieth century in the US, farmers were losing their farms because they had a lack of capital to invest in planting crops. The bankers who ran the economy insisted that the US not overspend. But at that time, there was more productive capacity in the economy than there was money to lubricate transactions and allow people to invest in making more economic activity happen.

Advocates of modern monetary theory are right that the fear of the deficit is a way that those advocating for the interests of the wealthy have fooled people into believing that what is good for them is good for everyone. Deficits can be much larger than many people believe. In the US at present, Republicans use fear of the deficit to thwart spending on public goods, even while they don't hesitate to increase the deficit to give tax cuts to the wealthy.

Proponents of MMT often overstate their case, though. One of the most troubling ways is in Kelton's book she doesn't distinguish what the US can do as the owner of the world's sovereign currency from what other countries that need dollars can do. Countries with weaker currencies can't simply print money to finance public goods. If they did, their currency would be devalued, and they would be able to buy less on the global market. When the US floods the market with dollars that has the impact on the currencies of other countries. MMT does a great job exploding the myths that drive austerity politics in the US, and to show the hypocrisy of Republican calls for cutting spending on social goods, but it is not a magic bullet for ending poverty or breaking dependencies on capitalism.

Guaranteed Basic Income

The most powerful way to make individuals less dependent on capitalism to survive is for the government to give them the money they need to live. While the idea of a GBI may seem far-fetched, in fact, many societies have systems of income support. In most European societies there is some system of welfare in place where people who are not able to work are given what they need to survive. Even more countries have some form of pensions for the elderly or for those unable to work because of disability. The US has an Earned Income Tax credit, also called a negative income tax, that goes to those too poor to pay income taxes.

Many societies have ways of getting money to low-income people. When there are work requirements associated with them, they are called conditional cash transfers. When there are no conditions attached, they are called Unconditional Cash Transfers (UCT). The most expansive approach to a GBI is the universal basic income (UBI).

The Basic Income Earth Network (BEIN) works to promote UBI, which it defines as having these five characteristics:

1 Periodic: distributed in regular payments
2 Cash payment: distributed as funds, not coupons or vouchers
3 Individual: paid to every adult citizen, not just every household
4 Universal: it is paid to all citizens, regardless of their situation
5 Unconditional: there are no requirements regarding employment status or any other criteria[27]

There are advantages and disadvantages to each of these approaches for supportive wealth transfers. US Senator Bernie Sanders prefers the negative income tax because the mechanisms for it are already in place, and the concept of using income tax to redistribute wealth is widely accepted and widely understood. Advocates of GBI and UBI argue that an advantage of their schemes is that people are given money regularly in the form of monthly payments and so it helps with cash flow. Advocates of UBI argue that it is better than a means tested approach, because it requires less bureaucracy to administer, and since everyone gets it, it has more broad support, and less stigma attached to it, than a program that only goes to the poor. The state of Alaska has had a UBI system in place since 1982. All adult Alaska residents receive an annual check for somewhere between $1,000 and 2,000 per year. At the height of the COVID-19 pandemic, the country of Togo offered a basic income to ensure that people had access to what they needed to survive in a period when there was not enough employment to ensure everyone's well-being.[28]

At the present time, many towns tine US are experimenting with a basic income support scheme where a small number of low-income people are given $500 per month to analyze the impacts it has on their well-being. The results of these experiments have been overwhelmingly positive. Generally, the people in these experiments have used the money to improve their lives in significant ways. Research on the impact of GBI programs globally has shown them to not disincentivize work, as conservative critics warn. And, not surprisingly, they lead to lower levels of poverty.

In a comprehensive review of the literature on GBI, Ioana Marinescu writes that,

> Multiple randomized controlled trials involving unconditional cash transfers have been conducted in developing countries. Unconditional cash transfers in a Kenyan experiment significantly increased consumption, especially on food, medical, and education items (Haushofer and Shapiro 2013). The pattern of spending by Kenyan households suggests that the cash transfers were able to alleviate credit constraints, allowing them to invest in assets people need to be productive, like livestock, which can increase earnings in the long term. More broadly, a review

of the literature concludes that unconditional cash transfers in developing countries do not increase expenditures on temptation goods, such as alcohol and tobacco.[29]

Many people work in at jobs producing, selling, and disposing of unnecessary consumer products. Many people work in industries, such as insurance and finance, that only are necessary in a poorly managed capitalist economy. If we move toward economies where people's needs are increasingly met through public goods and provisioning, and where there may be fewer jobs available, as automation increases, it makes sense to ensure that people have secure access to what they need to live. And when everyone has a GBI, it is much more difficult to make the claim that people should buy more things to keep people employed.

Political Movements for Enough

None of the policy changes argued for in this chapter are easy to achieve. All of them involve chllenging entrenched interests. In order to succeed at them we need to fight against the misleading ways of thinking that have people believing that what is good for the wealthy is good for all of us. We need to fight against ways of thinking that say that policy work is for someone else. And we need to simply fight. Work to raise the minimum wage is gaining ground as I write this. Some of the first to advocate for a $15 minimum wage were fast food workers who did that work outside of unions and often without support from any large well-funded organizations.

Some of my students were involved with a fight in San José to raise the minimum wage in the city through a ballot initiative in 2012. The student who started that work, Leila McCabe, started her organizing for it in a class at San José State University. She and her colleagues took their idea to a local labor organization which paid for a poll to see if it was a viable idea. After the poll showed positive results, unions then threw in the funding to support the work to pass the initiative. Their work helped build support for the movement that sprouted in many places and which has grown to national proportions since then.

All around the world, initiatives that end up being hugely consequential start as the small impossible ideas of a few people. When the right idea comes at the right time, and where there is a healthy ecosystem of organizations to support good work, and a media environment to amplify good ideas, our work can have substantial impacts. We can never know when our work is going to take off and be part of something larger, or when it will fizzle. But the work of organizing for a better world is nothing but the sum total of those efforts and the work done to create environments that help them have synergy.

Conclusion

Each of us can do many kinds of work to shift policies toward a world of enough. We can work for higher taxes that reduce inequality, we can work for the expansion of public goods, we can work for reduced work time. We can work to shift the stories we tell about who deserves to live well, and what living well looks like. We can work for regulations on gig work and to raise the minimum wage. We can work to elect politicians who will enact change, and we can help get people to believe that they deserve to vote. We can work against voter suppression. There is no magic bullet, or single best choice for where to put one's energy. Millions of people are working on these things, and anything we can do to contribute to them is enough.

Notes

1 A statement by trade unionist Nicholas Klein in 1918, often wrongly attributed ty Gandhi, https://www.professorbuzzkill.com/gandhi-first-they-ignore-you-then-they-laugh-at-you-then-they-fight-you-then-you-win-quote-or-no-quote/.
2 Heather McGhee. 2022. *The Sum of Us: What Racism Costs Everyone and How We Can Prosper Together.* One World.
3 Bill Moyer. 2001. *Doing Democracy: The MAP Model for Organizing Social Movements.* New Society.
4 Bill Moyer. 2001. *Doing Democracy: The MAP Model for Organizing Social Movements.* New Society.
5 The classic text exploring the power of disruption is Frances Fox Piven and Richard Cloward. 2012. *Poor People's Movements: Why They Succeed, How They Fail.* Vintage.
6 Mark Achbar and Jennifer Abbot, directors. 2004. *The Corporation.* See the film for an exploration of the ways that corporations check all of the boxes for the diagnosis of sociopath.
7 Kate Pickett and Richard Wilkinson. 2011. *The Spirit Level: Why Great Equality Makes Societies Stronger.* Bloomsbury, page 258.
8 Ira Katznelson. 2005. *When Affirmative Action Was White: An Untold History of Racial Inequality in Twentieth-Century America.* WW Norton & Company.
9 Warren Democrats. 2022. https://elizabethwarren.com/plans/ultra-millionaire-tax.
10 Bernie. 2022. https://berniesanders.com/issues/tax-extreme-wealth/.
11 Emmanuel Saez and Gabriel Zucman. 2019. "How would a progressive wealth tax work? Evidence from the economics literature." *Brookings Institution.*
12 Emmanuel Saez and Gabriel Zucman. 2019. "How would a progressive wealth tax work? Evidence from the economics literature." *Brookings Institution.*
13 Yanis Varoufakis. 2013. *The Global Minotaur: America, the True Causes of the Financial Crisis and the Future of the World Economy.* Zed Books.
14 Patrick Fleenor. 1994. "A History and Overview of Estate Taxes in the United States." The Tax Foundation, January. https://files.taxfoundation.org/legacy/docs/f7c34848582a114133f90711b50b9a3a.pdf.
15 Wikipedia Estate Tax. July 2022.
16 Anatole Anton. 2000. "Public Goods as Commonstock." In Anatole Anton, Milton Fisk, and Nancy Holmstrom, eds. *Not for Sale: In Defense of Public Goods.*

Westview Press, page 4. The concept of public goods is similar to the notion of the commons, but most people working on the idea of commons focus on things which are managed by self-regulating mechanisms separate from governments. Most theorists of the commons thinkers are opposed to the socialist idea of the government managing shared resources. The idea of public goods is therefore a broader concept. It includes self-managed as well as state-managed goods.

17 Nancy Holmstrom. 2000. "Rationality, solidarity, and public goods." In Anatole Anton, Milton Fisk, and Nancy Holmstrom, eds. *Not for Sale: In Defense of Public Goods*. Westview Press, pages 69–88.

18 Manuel Pastor. 2018. *State of Resistance: What California's Dizzying Descent and Remarkable Resurgence Mean for America's Future*. The New Press.

19 Heather McGhee. 2022. *The Sum of Us: What Racism Costs Everyone and How We Can Prosper Together*. One World, page 23.

20 Evan Bissell. 2019. "Notes on a Cultural Strategy for Belonging." Othering and Belonging Institute. https://belonging.berkeley.edu/notesonaculturalstrategy.

21 john a. powell. Forward to Evan Bissell. 2019. "Notes on a Cultural Strategy for Belonging." Othering and Belonging Institute, page 6. https://belonging.berkeley.edu/notesonaculturalstrategy.https://belonging.berkeley.edu/notesonaculturalstrategy.

22 Evan Bissell. 2019. "Notes on a Cultural Strategy for Belonging." Othering and Belonging Institute, page 33. https://belonging.berkeley.edu/notesonaculturalstrategy.https://belonging.berkeley.edu/notesonaculturalstrategy.

23 Evan Bissell. 2019. "Notes on a Cultural Strategy for Belonging." Othering and Belonging Institute, page 13. https://belonging.berkeley.edu/notesonaculturalstrategy.https://belonging.berkeley.edu/notesonaculturalstrategy.

24 Cynthia Kaufman. 2012. *Getting Past Capitalism: History, Vision, Hope*. Lexington Books.

25 Anders Hayden. 1999. *Sharing the Work, Sparing the Planet: Work Time, Consumption, & Ecology*. Zed Books.

26 Giorgos Kallis, Michael Kalush, Hugh O.'Flynn, Jack Rossiter, and Nicholas Ashford.
2013. ""Friday off": Reducing working hours in Europe." *Sustainability*, 5.4, 1545–1567. https://doi.org/10.3390/su5041545.

27 https://worldpopulationreview.com/country-rankings/countries-with-universal-basic-income.

28 Ted Alcorn. 2021. "One of the World's Poorest Countries Found a Better Way to Do Stimulus." November 7. *Bloomberg News*.

29 Ioana Marinescu. 2018. "No Strings Attached: The Behavioral Effects of US Unconditional Cash Transfer Programs." National Bureau of Economic Research (NBER), NBER Working Papers Series, Working Paper 24337, page 18. http://www.nber.org/papers/w24337.

Conclusion

Another world is possible, on a quiet day I can hear her breathing.
- Arundhati Roy

There is plenty in the world for all of us to have enough. But it will take an enormous amount of work to get to the place where all people get enough to live well and to find ways for people to feel that they have enough when they do. We can get to that world of enough by shifting resources to the poor. We get there by having those who actually have enough resist the status tugs that lead them to feeling unsatisfied when they have enough. We get there by reducing inequality. We get there by spreading narratives of the good life that aren't about consumption and waste. We need increased investment in the public goods that make people less dependent on consumerism for jobs: public transportation, free education, free health care, and low-cost housing. We need taxes on the wealthy and on luxury. We need work-time reduction in the form of higher minimum wages, an end to the exploitation of gig work, shorter work weeks, longer vacations, and more forms of paid time off. All of us have roles we can play in building a world of enough by doing individual work, cultural change work, and policy work.

We can build a world without poverty:

1 The world produces enough for everyone to live well and comfortably.
2 Poverty is caused by political choices to prioritize the interests of the wealthy for status goods, over the needs of the many to live well.
3 There are several kinds of policies that have been shown to reduce poverty: investment in public goods, ensuring that things people need to meet their basic needs are available at prices they can afford or by simply giving resources to those in need if they don't have the money to pay for them.

DOI: 10.4324/9781003354871-9

126 Conclusion

4 We need to measure poverty directly using the Multidimensional Poverty Index (MPI), and stop pretending that increased growth has a direct impact on poverty.
5 Taxes on the wealthy and transfers of funds from wealthy countries to poorer ones, transaction taxes, and debt relief are all mechanisms to redistribute funds downwards.
6 All around the world, in low-income countries and in wealthy ones, the means for eliminating poverty are well known. What is needed to eliminate poverty is the political work to change the policies that are causing harm.
7 We can all help eliminate poverty by spreading the idea that people have a basic human right to enough to live well, the idea that there is enough for everyone, and the idea that poverty is a choice made by those with political power. These ideas help build support for policies that eliminate poverty.

We can build a world of enough by helping those who have enough feel that they have enough:

1 Policies that lead to higher levels of equality are likely to lead to higher levels of happiness.
2 We can institute high taxes on the wealthy so we aren't always looking upward for status to people with absurd levels of wealth.
3 We need to elevate stories which give realistic views of why some people have more than others and bring back the stories that help explain and generate empathy for those who our social systems deprive of the resources they need to live well.
4 There is cultural work to be done making being a luxury consumer onto something that is socially stigmatized.
5 It is almost impossible for individuals to fight the pull of destructive forms of status without real policy changes to support those efforts.
6 Strengthening social fabric of relations by challenging race and gender-based system of oppression and increasing ways for people to feel a sense of belonging, and that give us sense of meaning and purpose outside of the consumer nexus, will help us to resist the pull to wasteful consumerism.
7 We can develop an aesthetics of well-being based on sufficiency.

We can work to radically shift how we think of economics:

1 Economic decisions need to focus on the three core criteria of enough: environmental sustainability, respect for human rights, and increased happiness for everyone.
2 No one should have unlimited wealth while others don't have what is needed for sufficiency.

3 Decisions about how to allocate resources need to take the ecological implications of decisions seriously.
4 When looking at economic questions we should think about how to create sufficiency and abundance, and how to manage scarcity fairly.
5 Policies that increase happiness should be preferred over ones that decrease happiness.
6 Economic thinking needs to take place in healthy dialogue with other disciplines and with open discussion of its underlying value-based assumptions. The economy needs to be understood as an aspect of a deeply interrelated social world. Economic thinking needs to take cultural history, values, and politics seriously.
7 We need to minimize the aspects of the economy that are based on the pursuit of profit.
8 We will be fighting an uphill battle against consumerism for as long as it is in the interest of powerful people and corporations to get us to want more.
9 Markets need to be embedded in other democratic social decision-making processes that hold those markets to account for generating good social outcomes.
10 We can promote ways to measure the success of an economy such as the Genuine Progress Indicator (GPI), which focuses on well-being, subtracts for things that are bad for society such as pollution, and adds for good things such as leisure.
11 We can challenge mainstream economic ideas wherever we encounter them. That can be in conversations, by commenting on the media we read and watch, by challenging the curricula at colleges and universities.

Capitalist modernity has helped create in people as sense that they are private citizens responsible for how they treat the people around them, and for the individual consumption choices they make, but not as contributors to our broader social world. The COVID crisis and the climate crisis have shown just how wrapped up in each other's lives we are. Each of us has some power to impact those larger forces. We can do that through cultural work and through policy work. We do cultural work by shifting the things we say to others, by living in subcultures that express different ways of living and by promoting alternative systems of meaning. We can all be cultural activists in many ways.

We can also all be policy advocates. For those of us who can vote, we can make a difference with our vote. People who are not eligible to vote can make a difference in the political system by supporting candidates who are committed to a world of enough and by fighting against voter suppression. Anyone can engage in work to lobby for a bill or to influence a politician. That is all an uphill battle as long as money dominates politics, so we can also work on campaign finance reform.

128 Conclusion

The concept of the Overton window says that at any given time there is a window of views on any given subject which are possible to enact in the political system. Some things are realistic and others are not. But what the history of social movements shows is that when there is enough of the right kinds of social disruption, the Overton window can shift dramatically and quickly. Think about how the summer of protest around murders of George Floyd and Breonna Taylor made defunding the police into a demand that was taken seriously in cities all around the US. While the police haven't been abolished, the movement led to police budgets being reduced for the first time in decades. All of us can engage in the social movements that add significant political pressure from the outside to world of electoral politics and so to shift what is possible for politicians to do.

Planet Earth is right now on a runaway train headed for destruction. One driver of that train is the insatiable desire for more that pushes people all around the world to seek after higher levels of unsatisfying consumption. Dominant economic theories, a culture that says more is better, a profit-driven economy that has people profiting from selling us things that are destined for the trash can, are driving an ecological crisis, all while leaving about a billion people in poverty, leaving even those who have a lot unhappy. Increasing numbers of people have clinical levels of anxiety and depression and have deep worries about the future.

What we need to do to stop that train is quite simple, even if it isn't easy. It is simple because we know how to ensure that there is enough for everyone. It is simple because the means for providing enough for everyone to live happy and comfortable lives are well within the possibilities of current productive technologies. It is simple because many economists have models for how to keep the engines of production running to produce enough, without relying on the unbridled capitalism that is producing the current crises.

But, of course, getting to a world of enough on time to avert the worst of the climate crisis is almost impossible, and it is very likely that we won't get there. Entrenched political forces are driving us to destruction. The engine of destruction is driven by several hundred-years' worth of propaganda that tells us that greed is good, that we should all live as private consumers, and that letting some people profit enormously from their private enterprises is necessary for us to produce the things we need. It is hard because our political systems are controlled by those same profit-driven forces. It is hard because people are led to believe that their well-being will come from their status-driven consumption. And it is hard because we lack the imagination to see that another world is possible.

But failure is really not an option for us as a species. We won't be able to make the atmosphere healthy as long as we are pushing our economies to produce more to buy and sell. The current system has generated misery for millions of people for the past 500 years, beginning in slavery and colonialism. Those who benefit from an extractive and exploitative economy are doing all they can to keep us from getting to a world of enough. Those forces are what is getting in the way of solving the climate crisis at the speed needed. We are at a moment were doing what is right for all of humanity is also what is necessary for our survival as a species. This doesn't mean that the wealthy will get on board with a transition to a world of enough. Already the world's billionaires are sending themselves into space for the fun of it, as the planet burns. And no matter who is the CEO of Exxon-Mobil, that corporation is programmed to be on a path of world destruction.

The more clarity we have about our roles in feeding that machine of destruction, the easier it will be to build a world of enough. The clearer we are about the policy paths that will shift us away from an addiction to consumerism, the easier it will be to build a world of enough. The more we understand and promote economic theories of sufficiency, the better positioned we are to build a world of enough. None of it is easy, but all of it is necessary for our survival. And if we do the right things in the coming period, we can do more than survive. We could actually build a world where everyone has the things they need for good and sustainable lives.

Works Cited

2000 Watt Society. https://www.2000-watt-society.org/.

Achbar, Mark and Jennifer Abbot, Directors. 2004. *The Corporation*.

Akerlof, George A. 1978. "The market for "lemons": Quality uncertainty and the market mechanism." *Uncertainty in Economics*. Cambridge, MA: Academic Press, pages 235–251.

Alcorn, Ted. 2021. "One of the World's Poorest Countries Found a Better Way to Do Stimulus." November 7. *Bloomberg News*.

Alkire, Sabina. 2020. "How Has Global Multi-dimensional Poverty Changed over the First Ten Years of Measurement?" *Business Fights Poverty*, July 28. https://businessfightspoverty.org/articles/how-has-global-multi-dimensional-poverty-changed-over-the-first-ten-years-of-measurement/.

Alperovitz, Gar. 2011. "The New-Economy Movement: A Growing Group of Activists and Socially Responsible companies Are Rethinking Business as Usual." *The Nation*, May 25, 2011.

Alston, Philip. 2020. "The Parlous State of Poverty Eradication." Human Rights Council. July 2.

Anton, Anatole. 2000. "Public goods as commonstock." In Anatole Anton, Milton Fisk, and Nancy Holmstrom, eds. *Not for Sale: In Defense of Public Goods*. Boulder, CO: Westview Press.

Bandawe, Chiwoza and Anneke Meerkotter. 2015. "Developing a conceptual framework against discrimination on the basis of gender identity." *Using the Courts to Protect Vulnerable People*, 149–161.

Bissell, Evan. 2019. "Notes on a Cultural Strategy for Belonging." Othering and Belonging Institute. https://belonging.berkeley.edu/notesonaculturalstrategy.

Block, Fred and Margaret Sommers. 2014. *The Power of Market Fundamentalism: Karl Polanyi's Critique*. Cambridge, MA: Harvard.

Bloomberg, Michael and Carl Pope. 2017. *Climate of Hope: How Cities, Businesses, and Citizens Can Save the Planet*. New York, NY: St. Martin's Press.

Brown, Adrienne Maree. 2019. *Pleasure Activism*. Oakland, CA: AK Press.

Brown, Clair. 2017. *Buddhist Economics: An Enlightened Approach to the Dismal Science*. London: Bloomsbury.

Cameron, Jenny and J.K. Gibson-Graham. 2003. "Feminising the economy: Metaphors, strategies, politics." *Gender, Place and Culture: A Journal of Feminist Geography*, 10.2, 145–157.

Works Cited

Crist, Eileen, Camilo Mora, and Robert Engelman. 2017. "The interaction of human population, food production, and biodiversity protection." *Science*, 356.6335, 260–264.

Daly, Herman. 1991. *Steady-State Economics: With New Essays*. Washington, DC: Island Press.

Daoud, Adel. 2011. "The modus vivendi of material simplicity: Counteracting scarcity via the deflation of wants." *Review of Social Economy*, 69.3, 275–305.

Daoud, Adel. 2018. "Unifying studies of scarcity, abundance, and sufficiency." *Ecological Economics*, 147, 208–217.

Darity Jr, William A. and A. Kirsten Mullen. 2020. *From Here to Equality: Reparations for Black Americans in the Twenty-First Century*. Chapel Hill, NC: UNC Press Books.

Davis, Mike. 2002. *Late Victorian Holocausts: El Niño Famines and the Making of the Third World*. Brooklyn, NY: Verso.

De Botton, Alain. 2008. *Status Anxiety*. New York, NY: Vintage.

Debt for Climate. https://debtforclimate.org/.

Dickinson, Tim. 2019. "Study: U.S. Fossil Fuel Subsidies Exceed Pentagon Spending." *Rolling Stone*, May 8. https://www.rollingstone.com/politics/politics-news/fossil-fuel-subsidies-pentagon-spending-imf-report-833035/.

Diener, Edward and Eunkook M. Suh, eds. 2003. *Culture and Subjective Well-Being*. Cambridge, MA: MIT Press.

Dinerstein, Eric, et al. 2019. "A global deal for nature: Guiding principles, milestones, and targets." *Science Advances*, 5.4, eaaw2869. https://www.science.org/doi/10.1126/sciadv.aaw2869.

Earl, Jake, Colin Hickey, and Travis N. Reider. 2017. Fertility, immigration, and the fight against climate change." *Bioethics*, 31.8, 582–589.

Edward, Peter and Andy Sumner. 2020. "The End of Poverty and the Politics of Measurement and Governance of Growth." *Global Policy*, July 15. https://www.globalpolicyjournal.com/blog/15/07/2020/end-poverty-politics-measurement-and-governance-growth.

Ehrlich, Paul R. and Anne H. Ehrlich. 2013. "Can a collapse of global civilization be avoided?" *Proceedings of the Royal Society B: Biological Sciences*, 280.1754, 20122845.

"Estate Tax in the United States." 2022. *Wikipedia, The Free Encyclopedia*, Wikimedia Foundation, July 28. https://en.wikipedia.org/wiki/Estate_tax_in_the_United_States.

Evans, Dale, Andrew McMeekin, and David Southerton. 2011. "Sustainable consumption, behaviour change policies, and theories of practice. *International Review of Behaviour Change Initiatives*. Edinburgh: The Scottish Government.

Falk, Johan, Owen Gaffney, et al. 2019. *Exponential Roadmap: Scaling 30 Solutions to Halve Emissions by 2030*. Version 1.5. https://exponentialroadmap.org/wpcontent/uploads/2019/09/ExponentialRoadmap_1.5_20190919_Single-Pages.pdf.

Fengyan, Tang, et al. 2019. "The race paradox in subjective wellbeing among older Americans." *Ageing & Society*, 39.3, 568–589.

Ferguson, Ann. 1989. *Blood at the Root: Motherhood, Sexuality, and Male Dominance*. London: Pandora.

Fleenor, Patrick. 1994. "A History and Overview of Estate Taxes in the United States." *The Tax Foundation*, January.

Folbre, Nancy. 2014. "The care economy in Africa: Subsistence production and unpaid care." *Journal of African Economies*, 23.suppl_1, i128–i156.

Frank, Robert H. 2001. *Luxury Fever: Why Money Fails to Satisfy in an Era of Excess*. New York, NY: Simon and Schuster.

132 Works Cited

Fthenakis, Vasilis, et al. 2022. "Comment on Seibert, MK; Rees, WE through the eye of a needle: An eco-heterodox perspective on the renewable energy transition. Energies 2021, 14, 4508." *Energies*, 15.3, 971.

Gardner, Dan. 2010. *Future Babble: Why Expert Predictions Fail – and Why We Believe Them Anyway.* Toronto: McClelland and Stewart.

Gates, Bill. 2021. *How to Avoid a Climate Disaster: The Solutions We Have and the Breakthroughs We Need.* New York, NY: Knopf, 2021.

Gibson-Graham, J.K. 1993. "Waiting for the revolution, or how to smash capitalism while working at home in your spare time." *Rethinking Marxism*, 6.2.

Gibson-Graham, J.K. 2007. *A Postcapitalist Politics.* Minneapolis, MN: University of Minnesota Press.

"Global Multidimensional Poverty Index 2019: Illuminating Inequalities." http://hdr. undp.org/sites/default/files/mpi_2019_publication.pdf.

Guardian. 2021. Editorial. "The Climate Crisis Is Just Another Form of Global Oppression by the Rih World." November 5. https://www.theguardian.com/commentisfree/2021/nov/05/the-climate-crisis-is-just-another-form-of-global-oppression-by-the-rich-world.

Gustin, Georgina. 2017. "25 Fossil Fuel Producers Responsible for Half Global Emissions in Past 3 Decades." July 9, *Inside Climate News.*

Hahn, Rachel. May 12, 2020. "These Moms Fought for a Home—And Started a Movement." *Vogue.* See also The Moms of Magnolia Street. https://www.youtube. com/watch?v=KZLqjTxSNVM.

Hawken, Paul D. ed. 2017. *Drawdown: The Most Comprehensive Plan Ever Proposed to Reverse Global Warming.* New York, NY: Penguin.

Hayden, Anders. 1999. *Sharing the Work, Sparing the Planet: Work Time, Consumption, & Ecology.* London: Zed Books.

Holmstrom, Nancy. 2000. "Rationality, solidarity, and public goods." In Anatole Anton, Milton Fisk, and Nancy Holmstrom, eds. *Not for Sale: In Defense of Public Goods.* Boulder, CO: Westview Press, pages 69–88.

Housegrail. https://housegrail.com/how-many-vacant-homes-are-there-us/.

Huber, Matthew T. 2022. *Climate Change as Class War: Building Socialism on a Warming Planet.* Brooklyn, NY: Verso.

Iceland, John. 2013. *Poverty in America: A Handbook* (3rd Edition). Berkeley, CA: University of California Press.

International Student Initiative for Pluralism in Economics. 2014 open letter http://www.isipe.net/open-letter.

Jacobson, Mark. https://web.stanford.edu/group/efmh/jacobson/.

Kallis, Giorgos, Michael Kalush, Hugh O.'Flynn, Jack Rossiter, and Nicholas Ashford. 2013. ""Friday off": Reducing working hours in Europe." *Sustainability*, 5.4, 1545–1567. https://doi.org/10.3390/su5041545.

Katznelson, Ira. 2005. *When Affirmative Action Was White: An Untold History of Racial Inequality in Twentieth-Century America.* New York, NY: WW Norton & Company.

Kaufman, Cynthia. 2012. *Getting Past Capitalism: History, Vision, Hope.* Blue Ridge Summit, PA: Lexington Books.

Kaufman, Cynthia. 2020. *Challenging Power: Democracy and Accountability in a Fractured World.* London: Bloomsbury.

Kaufman, Cynthia. 2021. *The Sea Is Rising and So Are We: A Climate Justice Handbook.* Oakland, CA: PM Press.

Works Cited

Keynes, John Maynard. 2016. "Economic possibilities for our grandchildren." In *Essays in Persuasion*. Berlin: Springer.

Kickel, Jason. 2019. "Bill Gates Says Poverty Is Decreasing. He Couldn't Be More Wrong." January 29. https://www.theguardian.com/commentisfree/2019/jan/29/bill-gates-davos-global-poverty-infographic-neoliberal.

Klöwer, Milan, et al. 2020. "An analysis of ways to decarbonize conference travel after COVID-19." *Nature*, 356–359.

Lakner, Christoph, et al. 2019. "How much does reducing inequality matter for global poverty." *World Bank Working Paper* 8869.

Layard, Richard. 2005. *Happiness: Lessons from a New Science*. New York, NY: Penguin.

Leyte, Richard, et al. 2019. "A comparative analysis of the status anxiety hypothesis of socio-economic inequalities in health based on 18,349 individuals in four countries and five cohort studies." *Scientific Reports*, 9.1, 1–12.

Loha, Tanuka. 2011 "Housing: It's a Wonderful Right." Amnesty International. December 21. https://blog.amnestyusa.org/us/housing-its-a-wonderful-right/.

MacLean, Nancy. 2018. *Democracy in Chains: The Deep History of the Radical Right's Stealth Plan for America*. New York, NY: Penguin.

Marinescu, Ioana. 2018. "No Strings Attached: The Behavioral Effects of US Unconditional Cash Transfer Programs." National Bureau of Economic Research (NBER), NBER Working Papers Series, Working Paper 24337, page 18. http://www.nber.org/papers/w24337.

Marx, Karl. 1978. "'The power of money in bourgeois society.' Economic and philosophical manuscripts of 1844." In Robert C. Tucker, ed. *The Marx-Engels Reader*. New York, NY: W.W. Norton.

Mayer, Jane. 2017. *Dark Money: The Hidden History of the Billionaires behind the Rise of the Radical Right*. London: Anchor.

Mbiti, John. S. 1990. *African Religions and Philosophy* (2nd Edition). Portsmouth, NH: Heinemann.

McGhee, Heather. 2022. *The Sum of Us: What Racism Costs Everyone and How We can Prosper Together*. London: One World.

McKibben, Bill, Diana Nabiruma and Omar Elmawi. 2021. "Let's Heed the UN's Dire Warning and Stop the East African Oil Pipeline Now." *The Guardian*, August 17.

Microeconomics. 2022. Elumen. These are the opening lines of a microeconomics textbook. https://courses.lumenlearning.com/wm-microeconomics/chapter/understanding-economics-and-scarcity/page 1.

Monbiot, George. 2009. "Stop blaming the poor. It's the Wally Yachters who are burning the planet." *The Guardian*, September 28. https://www.theguardian.com/commentisfree/cif-green/2009/sep/28/population-growth-super-rich.

Morris, William. 2004. "Hopes and fears for art. Lectures on art and industry." *The Collected Works of William Morris*. Volume 22. Chestnull Hill, MA: Adamant Media Corporation.

Morris, William. 2020. *How I Became a Socialist*. Ed. Owen Holland. Brooklyn, NY: Verso.

Mortimer-Sandilands, Catriona and Bruce Erickson. 2010. *Queer Ecologies: Sex, Nature, Politics, Desire*. Bloomington, IN: Indiana University Press.

Moyer, Bill. 2001. *Doing Democracy: The MAP Model for Organizing Social Movements*. Gabriola, British Columbia: New Society.

134 Works Cited

Nature. 2020. "An Analysis of Ways to Decarbonize Conference Travel after COVID-19." July 15.

Nghiishililwa, Fritz. 2021. "Why poverty persists in developing countries, especially in Africa: A case of institutional failure or poor leadership." "Global jurisprudential apartheid in the Emergent One World Government."In Artwell Nhemachena, Tapiwa Victor Warikandwa, and Howard Tafara Chitimira, eds. *Global Jurisprudential Apartheid in the Twenty-First Century: Universalism and Particularism in International Law.* Lexington Books, pages 343–368.

Nove, Alec. 1991. *The Economics of Feasible Socialism Revisited.* Cambridge: Cambridge University Press.

Omi, Michael and Howard Winant. 2014. *Racial Formation in the United States.* Abingdon: Routledge.

Pastor, Manuel. 2018. *State of Resistance: What California's Dizzying Descent and Remarkable Resurgence Mean for America's Future.* New York, NY: The New Press.

Phillips, Leigh and Michal Rozworski. 2019. *The People's Republic of Walmart: How the World's Biggest Corporations Are Laying the Foundation for Socialism.* New York, NY: Jacobin.

Pickett, Kate and Richard Wilkinson. 2011. *The Spirit Level: Why Great Equality Makes Societies Stronger.* New York, NY: Bloomsbury Press.

Piketty, Thomas. 2021. *Capital and Ideology.* Cambridge, MA: Harvard.

Pinsker, Joe. 2019. "Why Are American Homes So Big?" *The Atlantic.* September 12. https://www.theatlantic.com/family/archive/2019/09/american-houses-big/597811/.

Piven, Frances Fox and Richard Cloward. 2012. *Poor people's Movements: Why They Succeed, How They Fail.* New York, NY: Vintage.

Polanyi, Karl. 1944. *The Great Transformation.* Boston, MA: Beacon.

Pörtner, Hans-Otto, et al. 2022. "Climate Change 2022: Impacts, Adaptation and Vulnerability." *IPCC Sixth Assessment Report.*

Powell, John A. Forward to Evan Bissell. 2019. *"Notes on a Cultural Strategy for Belonging."* Othering and Belonging Institute. https://belonging.berkeley.edu/notesonaculturalstrategy.https://belonging.berkeley.edu/notesonaculturalstrategy.

Professorbuzzkill. A Statement by Trade Unionist Nicholas Klein in 1918, Often Wrongly Attributed to Gandhi. https://www.professorbuzzkill.com/gandhi-first-they-ignore-you-then-they-laugh-at-you-then-they-fight-you-then-you-win-quote-or-no-quote/.

Ratcliff, Anna. 2020. *World's Billionaires Have More Wealth Than 4.6 Billion People.* Oxfam International. https://www.oxfam.org/en/press-releases/worlds-billionaires-have-more-wealth-46-billion-people.

Raworth, Kate. 2017. *Doughnut Economics: 7 Ways to Think Like a 21st-Century Economist.* White River Junction, VT: Chelsea Green Publishing.

Rees, William. 2021. "A Note on Climate Change and Cultural Denial." https://populationmatters.org/news/2021/11/bill-rees-note-climate-change-and-cultural-denial.

Resnick, Stephen A. and Richard D. Wolff. 1987. *Knowledge and Class: A Marxian Critique of Political Economy.* Chicago, IL: University of Chicago Press.

Ridley, John. 2005. "A $10,000 Martini at the Algonquin Hotel." National Public Radio Morning Edition. March 1. RIPPES. http://www.ripess.org/what-is-sse/what-is-social-solidarity-economy/?lang=en.

Robinson, Cedric. 1983. *Black Marxism: The Making of the Black Radical Tradition.* London: Zed Press.

Works Cited 135

Robinson, Mary. 2019. *Climate Justice: Hope, Resilience, and the Fight for a Sustainable Future*. London: Bloomsbury.

Rosnick, David and Mark Weisbrot. 2007. "Are shorter work hours better for the environment?" *International Journal of Health Services*, 37.3, 405–417.

Saez, Emmanuel and Gabriel Zucman. 2019. "How Would a Progressive Wealth Tax Work? Evidence from the Economics Literature." Brookings Institution.

Sahlins, Marshal. 1972. *Stone Age Economics*. Berlin: de Gruyter.

Samuelson, Paul A. and William D. Nordhaus, W.D. 2001. *Economics* (17th Edition). Boston, MA: McGraw-Hill.

Sanders, Bernie. 2022. https://berniesanders.com/issues/tax-extreme-wealth/.

Schor, Juliet. 2008. *The Overworked American: The Unexpected Decline of Leisure*. New York, NY: Basic Books.

Schumacker, E.F. 1973. *Small Is Beautiful: A Study of Economics As If People Mattered*. New York, NY: Harper Collins.

Seibert, M.K. and W.E. Rees. 2021. "Through the eye of a needle: An eco-heterodox perspective on the renewable energy transition." *Energies*, 14.15, 4508.

Sen, Amartya. 1982. *Poverty and Famines: An Essay on Entitlement and Deprivation*. Oxford: Oxford University Press.

Shiva, Vandana. 2005. *Earth Democracy: Justice, Sustainability and Peace*. London: Zed Books.

Shor, Juliet. 1992. *2010. Plentitude: The New Economics of True Wealth*. New York, NY: Penguin.

Skidelsky, Edward and Robert Skidelsky. 2012. *How Much Is Enough? Money and the Good Life*. New York, NY: Penguin.

Smith, Adam. 2010. *The Theory of Moral Sentiments*. New York, NY: Penguin.

Stearns, Peter N. 2006. *Consumerism in World History: The Global Transformation of Desire*. New York, NY; and London: Routledge.

Stearns, Peter N. 2020. *Happiness in World History*. New York, NY; and London: Routledge.

Suzman, James. 2017. *Affluence without Abundance: The Disappearing World of the Bushmen*. Bloomsbury Publishing USA.

Tax Foundation. https://files.taxfoundation.org/legacy/docs/f7c34848582a114133f90711b50b9a3a.pdf.

Tutu, Desmond. "We Need an Apartheid Style Boycott to Save the Planet." April 10, 2014, *The Guardian*.

Ueppen, Jim and James W. Vaupel. 2003. "Broken Limits to Life Expectancy." *Science's Compass Policy Forum*. http://www.soc.upenn.edu/courses/2003/spring/soc621_iliana/readings/oepp02b.pdf.

USA Facts. https://usafacts.org/data/topics/people-society/poverty/public-housing/homeless-population/?msclkid=d59717ec356c19154f72751be43cb6f3.

Utting, Peter. 2015. *Social and Solidarity Economy: Beyond the Fringe*. London: Zed Books.

van Norren, Dorine E. 2020. "The sustainable development goals viewed through gross national happiness, Ubuntu, and Buen Vivir." *International Environmental Agreements: Politics, Law and Economics*, 20.3, 431–458.

Varoufakis, Yanis. 2013. *The Global Minotaur: America, the True Causes of the Financial Crisis and the Future of the World Economy*. London: Zed Books.

Vettese, Troy and Drew Pendergrass. 2022. *Half-Earth Socialism: A Plan to Save the Future from Extinction, Climate Change and Pandemics*. Brooklyn, NY: Verso.

Wadsworth, Tim and Philip Pendergast. 2021. "Race, ethnicity and subjective well-being: Exploring the disparities in life satisfaction among Whites, Latinx, and Asians." *International Journal of Wellbeing*, 11.2, 51–72.

Waring, Marilyn. 1990. *If Women Counted: A New Feminist Economics*. New York, NY: Harper Collins.

Warren, Elizabeth and Warren Democrats. 2022. https://elizabethwarren.com/plans/ultra-millionaire-tax.

World Population Review. https://worldpopulationreview.com/country-rankings/countries-with-universal-basic-income.

Index

Note: Page number followed by "n" refers notes.

absolute poverty 11–14, 21; *see also* poverty
aesthetics: minimalism 37; positive for enough 44; subcultures of 43; of sustainable world 45–47
Affluence without Abundance: The Disappearing World of the Bushmen (Suzman) 32
Affluent Society (Galbraith) 12
Affluenza (James) 34
Alkire, S. 92
Alston, P. 13
American Legislative Exchange Council (ALEC) 74
anti-consumerist consumerism 37–38; *see also* consumerism
anti-corruption measures 93
Anton, A. 112
Aristophanes: *Wealth* 28
Aristotle 7, 54

Basic Income Earth Network (BEIN) 121
Beer, S. 80
Bentham, J. 56
Biden, J. 111
Biden presidency in 2021 108
biology of status anxiety 31; *see also* status anxiety
Bisell, E. 116–117
Black poverty 29; *see also* poverty
Bloomberg, M. 14
Brave New World 11
Brown, A. M.: *Pleasure Activism* 40–41
Buddhism 7
buen vivir (living well) 7, 11
bus rapid transit (BRT) 48

Cáceres, B. 93
capitalism 45, 72–74; aesthetics in food cultures 46; challenging 74–78; defined 5, 71; economic dependency trap of 117–118; imperatives in 46; racial 4
capitalist modernity 24, 44, 127
Castro, X. 93
Challenging Power: Democracy and Accountability in a Fractured World (Kaufman) 82
civil rights movement 104–105
Climate Change as Class War (Huber) 76
climate crisis 1, 12, 15, 17, 19, 76–78, 94, 106, 128–129
community colleges 81, 113
Confucianism 7
conspicuous consumption 26–27, 31, 41
consumerism 24–26; anti-consumerist 37–38; wasteful 20
Consumerism in World History (Steans) 25
consumption: conspicuous 26–27, 31, 41; shifting of wasteful 47–51; spreading cultures of less 42–44; subcultures of 40–42
"Cool Biz" (program) 48
COVID-19 12, 42, 49–50, 73, 90, 121, 127
C-reactive protein (CRP) 31
Crist, E. 17, 18
cultural change 51–52
cultural systems 171
culture of poverty 29

Daly, H. 60, 95
Daoism 7

138 Index

Daoud, A. 38–39, 61
Darity, W. A.: *From Here to Equality: Reparations for Black Americans in the Twenty-First Century* 29
Davis, M.: *Late Victorian Holocausts: El Niño Famines and the Making of the Third World* 60
De Anza College 30, 48, 102
de Botton, A.: *Status Anxiety* 28
Debt for Climate 94
The Deficit Myth: Modern Monetary Theory and the Birth of the People's Economy (Kelton) 119
dehumanization 4, 114
Doing Democracy: The MAP Model for Organizing Social Movements (Moyer) 103, 105–106
Doughnut Economics: 7 Ways to Think Like a 21st-Century Economist (Raworth) 86
downshifting/downshifters: counterproductive 43; material privilege to 43; role in building a world of enough 42; wealthy people 38–40
Drawdown 17

Earl, J. 17
ecological economics 95–97
economic(s) 54–68; ecological 95–97; economist's attempts to save GDP 64–66; efficiency and markets 67–68; feminist critique 61–64; measuring the health of 64; rational maximizer who can never get enough 56–57; scarcity 54, 57–61; solidarity 83–86
economic growth 6, 8, 11, 13, 65, 90–91, 94
"Economic Possibilities for our Grandchildren" (Keynes) 32
The Economics of Feasible Socialism (Nove) 81
economy: feminist critique 61–64; global/world 18, 55; usage of 97–98
Edward, P. 90
efficiency 68; and markets 67–68
Ehrlich, A.: *The Population Bomb* 15
Ehrlich, P.: *The Population Bomb* 15
eliminating extreme poverty 90–92; *see also* extreme poverty
enough, building a life with 36–52; aesthetics of sustainable world 45–47; anti-consumerist consumerism 37–38;

individual change becoming cultural change 51–52; living joyfully in our bodies 44–45; shifting wasteful consumption 47–51; spreading cultures of less consumption 42–44; subcultures of consumption 40–42; wealthy people downshifting 38–40
enough, policies and politics 101–123; economic dependency trap of capitalism 117–118; estate taxes 111; guaranteed basic income 120–122; income tax 111; policy change 106–107; political movements for 122; public banking and MMT 119–120; public goods 111–113; racism and inequality 114–115; reducing inequality 107–108; shifting systems of meaning 115–117; social movements 103–106; taxing the rich 109; transaction taxes 110–111; wealth tax 109–110; work-time reduction 118–119
enough, psychology of 24–35; biology of status anxiety 31; conspicuous consumption 26–27; consumerism 24–26; inequality 32–33; meaning in life 32–33; "smart for one but dumb for all" 26–27; solutions to the problem of status anxiety 33–34; success 27–31
enoughness 96
environmental crisis 14–20
environmental justice 14, 19
An Essay on the Principle of Population (Malthus) 15
estate taxes 111
eudaimonia 7, 11
Evans, D. 47–48
extreme poverty 13–14; eliminating 90–92; ending in Global South 92–95; *see also* poverty

feminist critique/feminism 61–64
Ferguson, A. 64
Flores, F. 80
Floyd, G. 105, 128
Folbre, N. 62
Forman, D. 15
Frank, R. H.: *Luxury Fever: Why Money Fails to Satisfy* 26, 41
From Here to Equality: Reparations for Black Americans in the Twenty-First Century (Darity and Mullen) 29
From Twitter to Teargas (Tufecki) 105

Index 139

Galbraith, J. K.: *Affluent Society* 12
Gates, B. 14
Genuine Progress Indicator (GPI)
66, 67, 127
Georgescu-Roegen, N. 95
*Getting Past Capitalism: History, Vision,
Hope* (Kaufman) 4–5, 72–73
Gibson-Graham, J. K. 71; *A Postcapitalist
Politics* 63
Gini index 91
global economic crash of 2008 55
Goal Blue 50–51
Gramsci, A. 115
Gross Domestic Product (GDP) 8–9, 20,
62, 67; ecological economist's attempts
to save 64–66
growth: economic 8, 11, 20, 21, 91; GDP
65, 66; green 65; infinite 54–68;
modern capitalism 73; population 13
guaranteed basic income (GBI) 111, 118,
120–122

Half-Earth Socialism (Vitesse and
Pendergrass) 75–80
happiness 6–11, 118; downshifters 38;
economics 98
Happiness in World History (Stearns) 6, 8
Happiness: Lessons from a New Science
(Layard) 8
Harris, K. 93
hedonism 6, 11, 56
Hickel, J. 91
Hickey, C. 16, 17
Hispanic health paradox 10
Holmstrom, N. 112
homelessness 59–60
*How Much is Enough: Money and the Good
Life* (Skidelsky and Skidelsky) 7, 11
Huber, M. T.: *Climate Change as
Class War* 76; on industrial working
class 77
Human Development Index (HDI) 66

Iceland, J. 11
*If Women Counted: A New Feminist
Economics* (Waring) 62
income tax 108, 109, 111, 120–121
individual change 51–52
inequality: economic 33, 108; fighting
against 34; income 67; meaning and
32–33; political 11; racism and 114–115;
reduction 13, 91, 107–18; social

cohesion 8; social solidarity 10; in
society 9, 31, 33; socioeconomic 10

Jacobson, M. 18, 19
James, O.: *Affluenza* 34
Jameson, F. 4

Kaufman, C.: *Challenging Power:
Democracy and Accountability in a
Fractured World* 82; *Getting Past
Capitalism: History, Vision, Hope* 4–5,
72–73; *The Sea is Rising and So Are We:
A Climate Justice Handbook* 19
Kelton, S.: *The Deficit Myth: Modern
Monetary Theory and the Birth of the
People's Economy* 119
Kerner, O. 29
Keynes, M.: "Economic Possibilities for
our Grandchildren" 32
Kondo, M. 36–37

Lanker, C. 13, 90–91
*Late Victorian Holocausts: El Niño Famines
and the Making of the Third World*
(Davis) 60
Layard, R.: *Happiness: Lessons from a New
Science* 8
Layte, R. 31
living joyfully in our bodies 44–45
Lumumba, P. 93
Luxury Fever: Why Money Fails to Satisfy
(Frank) 26, 41

Malthus, T.: *An Essay on the Principle of
Population* 15
Marinescu, I. 121–122
markets 59; and efficiency 67–68, 112;
fundamentalism 63
Marx, K. 68, 74, 76
Marxists 82
McCabe, L. 122
McGee, H.: *The Sum of Us: What Racism
Costs Everyone and How We Can Prosper
Together* 114
McMeekin, A. 47–48
meaning: in life 32–33; shifting systems
of 115–117
Midas (King) 28
Modern Money Theory (MMT)
119–120
Monbiot, G. 16
Morris, W. 45, 46

140   Index

Moyer, B. 115; *Doing Democracy: The MAP Model for Organizing Social Movements* 103, 105–106
Moynihan, D. P.: *The Negro Family* 29
Mullen, A. K.: *From Here to Equality: Reparations for Black Americans in the Twenty-First Century* 29
Multidimensional Poverty Index (MPI) 91–92, 95

Nature 50
The Negro Family (Moynihan) 29
neo-Malthusianism 14, 15, 18
New Deal 108
Nghiishililwa, F. 93, 94
Nove, A.: *The Economics of Feasible Socialism* 81

Omar, I. 67
Overton window 105, 128

Paddock, P. 15
Paddock, W. 15
patient capital 86
Pendergrass, D. 81; *Half-Earth Socialism* 75, 79–80
Pickett, K.: *The Spirit Level: Why Great Equality Makes Societies Stronger* 33–34, 107
Piketty, T. 73
Pleasure Activism (Brown) 40–41
Plentitude: The New Economics of True Wealth (Shor) 66
Polanyi, K. 68
policy change 106–107
political inequality 11; *see also* inequality
political movements for enough 122; *see also specific entries*
Pope, C. 14
population: of beauty pageant 45; of elderly in US 113; life satisfaction of 66; reduction 15–18; target 18; well-being for 108; of world 18
The Population Bomb (Ehrlich and Ehrlich) 15
A Postcapitalist Politics (Gibson-Graham) 63
poverty 11–14; absolute 11–14, 21; Black 29; culture of 29; elimination of 12,

89–99; extreme 13–14, 90–95; relative 12, 31
powell, j. a. 114, 116
preindustrial societies 25
pronatalist policies 17
Proposition 30 101–102
provisioning 62–63, 67, 72, 79, 80, 86, 118
public banking and MMT 119–120
public goods 111–113, 124n16; developing 86, 92, 111–113; raising taxes to fund 101, 109, 111

race: class and 8, 10, 47, 113; gender and 33; politics of 115
racial capitalism 4
racism: challenging 113; inequality and 114–115; politics of ethno-nationalism and 34
rational maximizer 56–57, 59–60, 61
Raworth, K. 87; *Doughnut Economics: 7 Ways to Think Like a 21st-Century Economist* 86
Reagan Revolution 102
Real Simple 37
reducing inequality 13, 91, 107–18; *see also* inequality
Rees, W. 15, 16, 18
relative poverty 12, 31; *see also* poverty
renewable energy (RE) 16
Resnick, S. 71
Rieder, T. N. 16
Robinson, M. 62
Rosser, M. 91

Sanders, B. 109, 111, 121
scarcity 54, 57–61
scarcity, abundance, and sufficiency (SAS) 61
Schumacher, E. F.: *Small Is Beautiful: A Study of Economics as If People Mattered* 96
Science 17
The Sea is Rising and So Are We: A Climate Justice Handbook (Kaufman) 19
Seibert, M. 16, 18
Sen, A. 60
shifting systems of meaning 115–117
shifting wasteful consumption 47–51; *see also* consumption

Index 141

Shor, Juliet: *Plentitude: The New Economics of True Wealth* 66
Skidelsky, E.: *How Much is Enough: Money and the Good Life* 7, 11
Skidelsky, R.: *How Much is Enough: Money and the Good Life* 7, 11
Small Is Beautiful: A Study of Economics as If People Mattered (Schumacher) 96
"smart for one but dumb for all" 26–27
Smith, A. 112; *Theory of Moral Sentiments* 68
social cohesion 10
socialism 79–83; defined 71–72, 79
social movements 103–106
socioeconomic inequality 10
socioeconomic position (SEP) 31
solidarity economics 83–86
Southerton, D. 47–48
The Spirit Level: Why Great Equality Makes Societies Stronger (Pickett and Wilkinson) 33–34, 107
status anxiety: biology of 31; solutions to the problem of 33–34
Status Anxiety (de Botton) 28
staycations 49, 51
Stearns, P.: *Consumerism in World History* 25; *Happiness in World History* 6, 8
stigmatized others 116
Stoknes, P. E.: *Tomorrow's Economy: A Guide to Creating Healthy Green Growth* 65
success 27–31
Sumner, A. 90
The Sum of Us: What Racism Costs Everyone and How We Can Prosper Together (McGee) 114
sustainability/sustainable 95; aesthetic 45–47; development 84; environmental 3, 6, 87, 98, 113; world 19, 45–47
Sustainable Development Goals 13
Suzman, J.: *Affluence without Abundance: The Disappearing World of the Bushmen* 32

Tang, F. 10
tax(es): estate 111; to fund public goods 101, 109, 111; income 108, 109, 111, 120–121; rich 109; transaction 110–111; Ultra-Millionaire Tax 109; wealth 109–110
Taylor, B. 128
techno-optimism 14, 18
Theory of Moral Sentiments (Smith) 68
Tobin, J. 111
Tomorrow's Economy: A Guide to Creating Healthy Green Growth (Stoknes) 65
transaction taxes 110–111
Trump, D. 111
Tufecki, Z.: *From Twitter to Teargas* 105
Tutu, D. 4

ubuntu 7, 11
Ultra-Millionaire Tax 109
Unconditional Cash Transfers (UCT) 120
universal basic income (UBI) 80, 120–121
Universal Declaration of Human Rights 60
utility maximisers 56

Vitesse, T. 81; *Half-Earth Socialism* 75, 79–80

Waring, M. 63; *If Women Counted: A New Feminist Economics* 62
Warren, E. 109
2000-Watt Society 82
Wealth (Aristophanes) 28
wealth tax 109–110
wealthy people downshifting 38–40
Wilkinson, R.: *The Spirit Level: Why Great Equality Makes Societies Stronger* 33–34, 107
Wolff, R. 71
work-time reduction 118–119, 125

Zelaya, J. 93